W9-ATP-428

Candide
optimism demolished

❡

Twayne's Masterwork Studies
Robert Lecker, General Editor

Candide
optimism demolished

¶

Haydn Mason

Twayne Publishers • New York

Maxwell Macmillan Canada • Toronto

Maxwell Macmillan International • New York Oxford Singapore Sydney

Twayne's Masterwork Studies No. 104

Copyright © 1992 by Twayne Publishers

Twayne Publishers
Macmillan Publishing Company
866 Third Avenue
New York, New York 10022

Maxwell Macmillan Canada, Inc.
1200 Eglinton Avenue East
Suite 200
Don Mills, Ontario M3C 3N1

Macmillan Publishing Company is a part of the Maxwell Communication Group of Companies.

Library of Congress Cataloging-in-Publication Data

Mason, Haydn Trevor
Candide : optimism demolished / Haydn Mason.
p. cm. — (Twayne's masterwork studies ; no. 104)
Includes bibliographical references and index.
ISBN 0-8057-8085-8 (cloth). — ISBN 0-8057-8559-0 (paper).
1. Voltaire, 1694–1778. Candide. I. Title. II. Series.
PQ2082.C4M36 1992
843'.5—dc20

92-32663
CIP

The paper used in this publication meets the minimum requirements of American National Standard for Information Sciences—Permanence of Paper for Printed Library Materials, ANSI Z39.48-1984.

10 9 8 7 6 5 4 3 2 1 (alk. paper)

10 9 8 7 6 5 4 3 2 1 (pbk.: alk. paper)

Printed in the United States of America.

For Gilly

contents

note on the references and acknowledgments

The translated excerpts throughout are my own; they are based on the French edition of *Candide* edited by René Pomeau (Oxford: Voltaire Foundation, 1980), volume 48 of *The Complete Works of Voltaire*, to which all page citations refer. The main text used for Voltaire works is *Oeuvres complètes*, edited by Louis Moland, 52 volumes (Paris: Garnier, 1877–85), and is cited as Moland. The text used for other *contes* is *Voltaire: Romans et Contes*, edited by Frédéric Deloffre and Jacques Van den Heuvel (Paris: Gallimard, 1979); it is cited as Deloffre and Van den Heuvel. The text used for the letters is *Voltaire's Correspondence*, edited by Theodore Besterman (Geneva and Banbury, England: Voltaire Foundation), volumes 85–135 of *The Complete Works of Voltaire*, 1968–75; it is cited as D followed by the letter number.

Two acknowledgments must be made, with deep gratitude: first, to Mrs. Judith Hurley, who typed and retyped the text with great care and devotion; second, to my wife Adrienne. The book bears the latter's imprint throughout—her comments (always incisive, even though not always taken up), her advice on structure, style, and presentation. Whatever its defects, this study would have been poorer without her.

Voltaire at 24 years of age. Portrait by Nicolas de Largillière. Versailles Château Museum.

chronology:
Voltaire's life and works

1694   Voltaire born, probably just outside Paris, as François-Marie Arouet, son of a high official in the Cour des Comptes (audit office).

1703–1711   Attends Jesuit college of Louis-le-Grand.

1710   Gottfried Leibniz's *Theodicy* is published. This work, offering, as the title implies, a vindication of God's justice and benevolence in view of the existence of evil, will have considerable influence, directly and indirectly, upon the discussion regarding optimism during the eighteenth century.

1715   Louis XIV dies; Louis XV succeeds to the throne. As he is still a child, France will be governed by the regency of the duke of Orléans until 1723.

1716   Already in trouble with the authorities, Voltaire is exiled to Sully-sur-Loire from May to October, accused of writing a satire upon the regent.

1717   Imprisoned in May in the Bastille for 11 months on account of another satire.

1718   Begins using the name of Voltaire in June, thereby rejecting the detested family name. His first play, *Oedipe*, is staged in November establishing him as the foremost tragic dramatist in France until his death 60 years later.

1723   *La Ligue* (later given the definitive title *La Henriade*) is published. This epic poem enjoys great popularity.

1725	Voltaire is at the height of his success in Paris and at the court of Versailles. Three of his plays are performed as part of the celebrations of Louis XV's marriage. He receives a pension from the queen.
1726	He quarrels in January with the Chevalier Rohan, scion of one of the leading families of France, at the Opéra and is subsequently beaten by the Chevalier's servants. Voltaire's rage is boundless, but he discovers that, in a row between a bourgeois and a true aristocrat, however popular the former, the latter will win the support of his powerful friends. Voltaire contemplates a duel and begins fencing lessons to that end. Considered a threat to public order, he is arrested and once more placed in the Bastille. He is released a month later on condition that he leave Paris. He decides to go to England, arriving in London in May.
1728	Leaves England in November; spends winter in Dieppe.
1733	Alexander Pope's *Essay on Man* is published. Voltaire will retain his admiration for the poem, but in later years, especially after 1755, he will become unhappy with its affirmation of optimism.
1734	*Lettres philosophiques* is published in France in April and is immediately condemned by the Parlement of Paris; a warrant is issued for the author's arrest on account of the work's offensive comments upon politics and religion. Voltaire goes into hiding, eventually settling at Cirey, home of his mistress, Madame du Châtelet.
1735	Is allowed to return to Paris but continues to live mainly at Cirey.
1736	Begins correspondence with Frederick of Prussia (later Frederick II).
1738	*Discours en vers sur l'homme* is published.
1744	Beginning of love affair with his niece, Madame Denis.

1745   In April, appointed historiographer to Louis XV at Versailles.

1746   Elected to Académie Française in April (after one previous failed attempt in 1743).

1747   *Zadig* (under original title of *Memnon*), the first of Voltaire's *contes*, is published in June. His period of favor at the court ends in October when indiscretions oblige Voltaire and Madame du Châtelet to flee Versailles.

1749   Madame du Châtelet dies suddenly in September at Lunéville; Voltaire, still her companion, is stunned by her death.

1750   In June, accepts Frederick's invitation to join him in Berlin. Voltaire will not see Paris again until three months before his death.

1752   Quarrels with his compatriot Maupertuis, president of the Academy of Berlin, at Frederick's court. Publishes a virulent satire on Maupertuis, *Diatribe du docteur Akakia*, which is publicly burned, on Frederick's orders. *Micromégas* is published.

1753   His deepening rift with Frederick leads to Voltaire's departure from Berlin in March. Voltaire and Madame Denis are forcibly detained by Frederick's officials in June at Frankfurt for five weeks. Voltaire settles in October in Colmar, which becomes his center for the next twelve months.

1754   Learns that he is persona non grata to Louis XV in Paris because of his departure to live at Frederick's court. He also discovers that Frederick does not want him back either. Begins looking for a permanent residence in the area of Geneva or Lausanne.

1755   In January, purchases Les Délices in Geneva, his main home for the next three years. Forbidden by Genevan authorities in July to put on plays at Les Délices. Earthquake strikes Lisbon on 1 November.

1756   *Essai sur les moeurs,* one of his major historical works, is published. *Poème sur le désastre de Lisbonne* is published. Frederick II invades Saxony in August, thereby starting the Seven Years' War.

1757   Robert Damiens attempts to assassinate Louis XV in January. Admiral John Byng is shot in March. Frederick II is victorious over the French in November at the battle of Rossbach. Volume 7 of the *Encyclopédie,* including the notorious article "Genève," is published in November. The ensuing scandal—which arises because of "Genève," written mainly by Jean d'Alembert with some contributions by Voltaire—leads to a suspension of publication of the whole enterprise and resignation of d'Alembert as one of the two editors. (Denis Diderot, his co-editor, will, however, remain to see the *Encyclopédie* through to eventual completion in 1765.)

1758   Visits Schwetzingen, home of the Elector Palatine near Mannheim, in July for a stay of five weeks. In October, purchases Tournay, near Geneva. Claude Helvétius's *De l'esprit* is published.

1759   *Candide* is published in Paris in January or February. In February, Voltaire purchases Ferney, near Geneva, henceforth to be his home. *Mémoires* written (published posthumously).

1762   In April, begins his campaign to rehabilitate the memory of Jean Calas, a merchant of Toulouse who had been executed in March on dubious evidence for allegedly killing his son. The campaign, conducted with great vigor over the ensuing years, will result in a complete reversal of the verdict in 1765. This is but the most renowned of a whole series of defenses against miscarriages of justice and of polemical writings that will occupy Voltaire for the rest of his life. Comes to be known as *l'homme aux Calas.*

1763   Seven Years' War ends. Treaty of Paris is signed.

1764   *Dictionnaire philosophique* is published.

1766   The chevalier of La Barre, a young man aged 19, is burned at the stake in July in Abbeville for sacrilege and blasphemy. Voltaire is horrified at the disproportion between the crime and the penalty, and he is filled with a new revulsion for the barbarism still practiced by French authority. He considers fleeing from France and founding a colony for *philosophes* in Frederick's Prussia, at Cleves. But his fellow writers in Paris are unwilling to move, particularly Diderot, and Voltaire is obliged to abandon the scheme. *Le Philosophe ignorant* is published.

1767   *L'Ingénu* is published. This *conte*, considered generally to be, with *Zadig*, Voltaire's most important after *Candide*, is a fierce attack upon religious persecution and intolerance in France.

1767–1772   Voltaire's philosophical crusade against injustice reaches its height in an outpouring of works of every kind: satires, epistles, tragedies, stories, dialogues, pamphlets, dictionary articles.

1774   Louis XV dies, to be succeeded by Louis XVI. It gradually becomes apparent that no formal order excluding Voltaire from Paris has ever been issued and that therefore he is free to return to the capital if he so wishes.

1775   Pierre Beaumarchais's *Le Barbier de Séville* is first put on at the Comédie Française in February.

1776   American War of Independence begins.

1778   Voltaire returns to Paris in February, to a delirious welcome. In a virtual apotheosis during his own lifetime, he is greeted, over the next few weeks, by special deputations from the Académie Française and the Comédie Française, meets Benjamin Franklin and blesses the latter's grandson, and is crowned by the actors of the Comédie Française when he attends a performance of his tragedy *Irène*. But he is taken seriously ill and dies 30 May. Since he has not made a religious end to his life, he cannot be buried in consecrated ground in Paris. So his body is smuggled out of the capital by night and interred at Scellières, in Champagne.

1791   Voltaire's remains are brought back to Paris in July to be placed in the Panthéon, after a solemn procession of great magnificence.

Literary and
Historical Context

❡

1

The Context

The problem of evil, which is at the heart of *Candide* (1759), had long troubled Voltaire. Why is there suffering in the world? Why are human beings malicious toward one another? Why disease, pain, hunger? Why greed, cruelty, and warfare? The questions took on an increasingly somber tone as Voltaire grew older, especially from the 1750s onwards. His own personal life had been darkened by the death of his former mistress, Madame du Châtelet, who to the day she died in 1749 remained a close companion and friend. Her sudden departure left him devastated for a while. He had lost, he said, "half of myself" (D-4024). There was suddenly, after 15 years of living with her, a void. Voltaire filled it by joining the court of the Prussian king, Frederick the Great, in Berlin. For a while things went well, but the experience was to end less than three years later in a bitter quarrel with Frederick, leading to Voltaire's withdrawal under a cloud of mutual suspicion. Humiliatingly detained for a month at Frankfurt by Frederick's officials, he was left, on his release, with no clear home to head for. He could not return to Paris since Louis XV had indicated that his departure from France to Prussia had made his presence unwelcome to the French king. Nearly two years were to pass before Voltaire found a new permanent home, in Geneva. It was a time of disillusion and uncertainty.

With his arrival in Geneva, however, Voltaire's fortunes began to improve. He bought Les Délices, a fine town house (today the home of the Voltaire Museum and Institute), where at first he

3

hoped he would live and die in peace, if fate allowed. For a time he was happy with Geneva. But here too disaffection was to set in. The Protestant pastors had been among those extending a warm welcome when he arrived, and Voltaire thought he had discovered a band of Christians as enlightened as their religion would allow. He was to learn otherwise. Late in 1757 appeared volume 7 of the *Encyclopédie*, the great philosophical dictionary being edited in Paris by Denis Diderot and Jean d'Alembert. This volume contained an article, "Genève," written by d'Alembert but with much help from Voltaire. It expressed Voltaire's view that the Genevan pastors' beliefs were almost devoid of Christian tenets such as the divinity of Christ or the eternity of hell.

The wrath of the pastors can easily be imagined. Whatever their precise personal beliefs, such a description was wholly scandalous. Voltaire's part in the article was well known. In addition, d'Alembert had expressed regret that regular theater was forbidden in Geneva, even in private homes. Here too Voltaire's hand could be clearly discerned. A passionate lover of theater, he had in his early months in Geneva put on performances at Les Délices, until the authorities banned them. The theater question also aroused hostile reaction, notably from Jean-Jacques Rousseau, whose *Lettre à d'Alembert sur les spectacles* on the subject, appearing in May 1758, remains one of that author's major works. The *Lettre* ensured that theater would be kept out of Geneva for more than 20 years.

So Voltaire's satisfaction with Geneva had vanished by the beginning of 1758. Once more the search for a new home was begun. He thought of Lorraine, where Madame du Châtelet had died; he put out new feelers about a return to Paris. But he was to learn that Louis XV's approval, required for either move, was definitively withdrawn. Voltaire, it seemed, would never again see his birthplace; he was to be forever cut off from the cultural center of his life.

The dark mood brewing at this time is probably not irrelevant to the composition of *Candide*. Other, public disasters added their quota. In November 1755 Voltaire learned of the great earthquake earlier that month at Lisbon, where at first it was thought that as many as 100,000 people had perished. His immediate reaction was to see the catastrophe as an unanswerable argument against philosophical optimism. His shock and horror found immediate expres-

sion in the philosophical *Poème sur le désastre de Lisbonne* (1756),
a work of 180 verses even in the first version, which was written in
the space of a week. The poem is aimed directly at the optimists'
view of the world, as the subtitle makes clear: "Examination of the
Axiom, *All is well.*" He assaults these complacent philosophers with
questions: What explanation have they to offer? Was the earthquake the result of necessary laws? How then can these laws
constrain a God both good and free? Or was it divine revenge? In
which case, was Lisbon more sinful than London or Paris? The
argument broadens to embrace a picture of the universal suffering
of human beings and animals alike. Even worse, there is universal
slaughter: the predatory vulture falls victim to the eagle, who is
shot by man, himself at the mercy of his fellowmen on the battlefield, his body becoming carrion for rapacious birds. Thus Voltaire
arrives at the central statement of the poem: "One has to accept,
evil is on the earth."

Voltaire's reaction to the Lisbon disaster, though profound,
was relatively ephemeral once he had expressed his pessimistic
outlook in verse. But the view of optimism had come to stay. It
would be reinforced in more lasting fashion when in 1756 the
Seven Years' War began. War, which the *philosophes* regarded as
probably the greatest of all scourges laid upon the human race, was
quickly seen by him as a decisive refutation of optimism. He was
appalled at the desolation wrought by Frederick's armies after they
had turned the tide in their favor with the decisive engagement at
Rossbach in November 1757. He was dismayed by the piratical
methods of the British navy on the high seas, capturing French
vessels in which Voltaire himself had considerable investments,
especially the fleet sailing from Cadiz. He intervened, unsuccess-
fully, with the British government to save Admiral John Byng's life
after the latter's ill-starred action against the French forces. "Your
sailors are not polite," he wrote (in English) to an Englishman in
1757 (D-7162). To his friend the duchess of Saxony-Gotha, who
while being in the thick of the war yet tried to discover reasons for
optimism from it, he commented sardonically: "We cannot yet say
'All is well,' but it is not going badly, and with time Optimism will
be conclusively demonstrated" (D-7297).

What, then, is optimism? It is, says Candide, "the mania for
asserting that all is well when one is not." Voltaire is drawing on

two different philosophical versions of optimism, one deriving from the German philosopher Gottfried Leibniz, the other from the English poet Alexander Pope. The apparent unrelatedness of these two thinkers may at first seem surprising, until one sees that it was a typical phenomenon of the period. From the early seventeenth century on, a new age of rationalism sprang up over Western Europe, with René Descartes as its progenitor and Benedict de Spinoza and Gottfried Leibniz as illustrious epigones in the tradition. After Descartes, confidence in reason as a reliable human instrument was renewed, and it was felt that reason could surely try to explain evil and suffering. Leibniz's *Theodicy* (1710) is the most distinguished attempt at a response. Leibniz wanted to save human beings from despair; reason, properly used, could lead to enlightenment. So he begins his large justification. He admits right away that evil exists. But evil is always a negative thing, never God's will. There is more good than evil; God is infinite, the Devil is not. However, the essential truth, as Leibniz sees it, is that there are laws of "sufficient reason" in the universe. Even God could not make 2 and 2 add up to 5, or create a spherical cube. So He was obliged, in creating a world, to choose between models all of which were flawed from the outset. In the end, He chose for our earth the best possible world, the one containing the greatest amount of variety and richness within the limitations imposed by necessity.

Leibniz's philosophy was taken up after his death by a disciple, Christian Wolff, who systematized it into an imposing philosophical structure that, since the late 1730s, was being translated into French. Voltaire doubtless got to know it, at least in extracts, through Madame du Châtelet, who was a convinced Leibnizian. In 1744 he wrote a letter to another disciple, Martin Kahle, in which for the first time he expressed a clear dislike for "the best of all possible worlds" (D-2945). Doubts about the nature of providence occur in the first published *conte, Zadig* (1747), but the plot suggests that in the end a wise man, like the hero, will find happiness, despite many tribulations and the presence of incomprehensible evils in the world. Between *Zadig* and *Candide*, Voltaire resolved his hesitations about optimism in taking up an attitude of hostility toward the doctrine.

Pope's philosophical viewpoint is much less thoroughgoing. It is expressed in his *Essay on Man* (1733) in lines such as these:

All Nature is but Art, unknown to thee;
All Chance, Direction which thou canst not see;
All Discord, Harmony not understood;
All partial Evil, universal Good:
And, spite of Pride, in erring Reason's spite,
One truth is clear, "Whatever is, is RIGHT."[1]

There is no recognition here of the existence of evil; it is simply "Harmony not understood," part of a universal good in which everything that is present in the world is justly so. Where Leibniz urges his readers to go on improving themselves morally, Pope advocates total submission—what Albert Camus, in our century, would define as "saying Yes to the universe."[2]

It is this more superficial version of optimism that Voltaire had in mind when he came to compose *Candide*. His reaction to the Lisbon earthquake bears this out. In a letter of the time he stated that his poem about that disaster attacks "Pope's principle that all that is, is well" (D-5952); the notes he appended to the poem make clear that he was far more attentive to Pope than to Leibniz. None of this has basically changed in *Candide*. It has been pointed out that the references to Leibniz are, with one exception (the reference in chapter 22 to evil being as shadows to a fine painting), unspecific. There is no evidence that at the time of *Candide* Voltaire had read Leibniz with any great care.

Why then, it must be asked, is *Candide* not an onslaught on Pope rather than on Leibniz? While no clear-cut answers may be given to this question, certain hypotheses may be advanced with some confidence. First, Voltaire admired Pope, as he did not admire Leibniz. For all its depressingly fatalistic attitudes to evil, the *Essay on Man* contains, in Voltaire's view, high moral and spiritual qualities. The preface to the *Poème sur Lisbonne* makes that clear, as does a 1756 addition to the *Lettres philosophiques* (1734) in which Voltaire describes Pope's work as "the finest didactic poem, the most useful, the most sublime ever written in any language."[3] It would have been wrong, therefore, to devastate such a masterpiece because of its one weakness. By contrast with Pope, Leibniz was without value: a purely speculative metaphysician, without relevance to the realities of the world. Besides, Voltaire seems to have known Leibniz, at least at this time, only through the presentation of his work by Wolff, who produced it under such titles as *Logic*,

Cosmology, and *Natural Theology*—an irresistible target for such barbs as the "metaphysico-theologo-cosmolonigology" that Pangloss is teaching in Westphalia. Furthermore, Leibniz, unlike Pope, had developed a philosophical jargon in which phrases like "sufficient reason" and, above all, "the best of all possible worlds" held sway. What better material for Voltaire's satiric pen? Instead of taking on an admired poet from a country that Voltaire generally respected (England, significantly, almost entirely escapes punishment in the universal denunciation that is *Candide*), Voltaire found it to be much more straightforward to situate the home of optimism in Germany: backward, provincial, unenlightened.

2

The Importance of Candide

Why, then, has *Candide* become so popular—the one work by Voltaire to have taken an undisputed place among the world classics? After all, the belief in Leibnizian optimism that is its ostensible target is no longer in the forefront of our thinking. Constant exposure to the media, with unremitting reports of AIDS, earthquakes, and massacre, has long since acquainted us with the sense that this world is very far from the best possible; we do not need to read *Candide* to discover that. As Aldous Huxley put it, nearly 70 years ago, "The wisdom of Martin and the Old Woman who was once betrothed to the Prince of Massa-Carrara has become the everyday wisdom of all the world since 1914." Huxley went on: "Then came the war. . . . We have discovered, in the course of . . . the last seven years, that astonishment is a supererogatory emotion. All things are possible, not merely for Providence, whose ways we had always known . . . to be strange, but also for men."[1] Those words would still hold good today, with the sole difference that since the 1920s we have discovered even more horrors of which man is capable.

So it is not documentary evidence that we seek in *Candide*. What Voltaire provides is a whole worldview, unique and self-consistent, and this view remains as relevant today as it was in 1759. Voltaire's own prolonged questioning over the problem of evil, which troubled him more immediately than it did any of the other great French writers of the eighteenth century, had led him up to this masterpiece. At last he had been forced to recognize unequivocally that the world contains evil beyond our capacity to in any way justify or explain by the light of our human understanding. But others had done so before Voltaire. Shock at the scandal of suffering and injustice is admirable. Such a reaction, however, is a common enough experience of sensitive souls, and it does not of itself make for great art.

Voltaire's achievement was to show that human existence as he saw it was irredeemably comic. It is not the cheerful comedy of Pierre-Augustin Caron de Beaumarchais's *Le Barbier de Séville* (1775), still less of Pierre de Chamblain de Marivaux's *Le Jeu de l'amour et du hasard* (1730). But Voltaire had the genius to see that, for him, the posturing gestures of human beings on our little ant heap, as he describes the world in his correspondence, are the very stuff of humor. For human beings are not simply overwhelmed by fate, as a tragic attitude would suggest. Nor do they possess some God-given kind of dignity, as a Christian might suppose. The world is full of evil, undeniably, as Voltaire goes all out to demonstrate from the very first in *Candide*. But it is also tolerable. More than that, human beings are free, or—amounting to the same thing in practical terms—they act as though they were free. They do not simply react, like billiard balls or cameras, to stimuli. They contain a bewildering capacity for disinterested good, though not, it is true, very often or very widely. More often, they are gratuitously murderous or deceitful. The world is not a happy place, and the simple pursuit of happiness can be naïve and discouraging. There is no pot of gold at the end of the rainbow.

Candide, though it reads like a fantasy, is firmly rooted in reality and in historical events, as we have seen. Voltaire constantly reminds us that the Seven Years' War and its atrocities are a present reality, that princes have been overthrown and often put to death ever since Old Testament Israel, that syphilis and prostitution rage throughout the world. Thus the fictional wickedness of Vanderdendur or the stupidity of the young Baron is entirely believable because these ways of behaving have their counterparts in the world around us. Nor are malice and injustice the only burdens we have to carry; worse, if anything, is the threat of boredom. When human beings find momentary rest from harassment, they may well fall victim to the demon of torpor, the sense that every experience, even the most cultivated, lacks any savor. Long before

Baudelaire, Voltaire had seen that human life risks oscillating between ennui and rage, unless we try to find a way of coming to terms with the predicament.

Moreover, this is a universal picture, not just one of Geneva or Paris writ large. Voltaire's classical view of human nature as fundamentally the same the world over beneath the superficial differences of custom between one country and another is brought to bear on what is constant and enduring in the human condition. That is why *Candide* addresses itself so easily to us more than 200 years later.

But this is not all. Human beings are not only greedy, treacherous, and unpredictable, but also delightfully foolish, even mad. For they surround themselves with systems of belief to keep the sense of evil at bay. The propensity of human beings to find consolation in even the most tragic circumstances is one of the basic aspects of our nature. There is nothing at all incredible about Candide's wish to believe that the desolation caused by the battle at sea finds a meaning in the death of the villain Vanderdendur. Human nature is readily prone to finding "lessons" in disasters because any system of order to which we may appeal seems better than no system at all. Such a failure to see suffering for what it is can be tragic; Henrik Ibsen's *The Wild Duck* (1884) is, for example, a case in point. But its failure can also be richly comic, if the perspective is changed. For the foolishness of Candide will not lead to ultimate despair. There has always been hope to keep him going, and when the naïveté of that hope has been finally exposed, he discovers that there still remains something to be tried, however uncertain the outcome. Human beings look forward, they have projects, they leave death out of account so long as the life force burns strongly in them. In brief, they act as though they were eternal. It is a comic spectacle, but the comedy is grounded in compassion and a deep sense of the injustice in human society.

Finally, *Candide* is not just a vision of the world. It is also a style. Brilliantly ironic, it is the ideal form of expression. It probes with limpid clarity the unclarity of human behavior and reasoning. It erects antithesis and balance to convey disorder and imbalance. The *conte* is, in this sense, pure paradox, so as to give its proper expression to a world that, as Voltaire put it elsewhere, "exists on contradictions."[2]

3

Critical Reception

We do not know exactly when *Candide* was published. Because it was going to scandalize authority, it would have to appear clandestinely and under a cloak of anonymity, as so many of Voltaire's earlier, also troubled works had done. (The original title made out that it was "translated from the German by Dr. Ralph.") We do know, however, that in mid-January 1759 Voltaire's publisher, Gabriel Cramer, sent 1,000 copies of *Candide* to Paris. We also know that by 22 February at the latest the work was selling in the French capital. Inevitably, it was received with disfavor by authority. The police officer responsible for investigating clandestine literature, Joseph d'Hémery, described it as "a bad joke on all countries and their customs."[1] The anonymity of authorship availed Voltaire nothing; he was already named in this early reference. D'Hémery's unflattering remarks were surpassed two days later by Advocate-General Omer Joly de Fleury, who had, not too surprisingly, discovered elements "contrary to religion and morals" (57). A police operation got under way at once to seize all the copies of *Candide* that could be found. But, as was often the case in the eighteenth century, official repression had not the means to cope with a popular work of literature. By the beginning of April Voltaire was speaking of the six editions that the *conte* had gone through. Before the year 1759 was out *Candide* had run to at least 17 editions (and in reality probably many more now lost) and had also been translated into English (three times over) and Italian.

The tale appeared not only in Paris but also in Geneva, London, and Amsterdam, and probably also in Lyon and Avignon. Voltaire and his publisher had evidently intended the appearance of *Candide* to be a European phenomenon, not just an event for the French capital alone. René Pomeau, in his authoritative edition, speculates that the 1759 editions may have amounted in total to 20,000 copies (64). For the period, that is a best-seller figure.

Conservative opinion followed the reaction of the authorities. The Genevan pastors denounced *Candide* as "full of dangerous principles concerning religion and tending to moral depravation" (65). It was a common reaction to see Voltaire as subversively presenting an odious picture of the world. Voltaire's enemy Elie Catherine Fréron, for example, suggested that "*Candide* first arouses the mind, but eventually strikes despair into the heart."[2] This view was echoed by the poet Edward Young, who replied directly to *Candide* in 1762 in a poem entitled *Resignation:*

> With so much sunshine at command,
> Why light with darkness mix?
> Why dash with pain our pleasure?[3]

No one was to voice this criticism better than Madame de Staël at the turn of the century. *Candide*, she maintained, was a "work of infernal gaiety," written by an author who laughs "like a demon, or like a monkey at the miseries of this human race with which he has nothing in common."[4] The *conte* was equally troublesome on literary grounds. Friedrich Melchior von Grimm, reviewing it in his *Correspondance littéraire*, refused to take it seriously. It was, he agreed, amusing, but it was devoid of all structure, all plan. Besides, it was full of indecencies. In short, it lacked any wisdom or mature reflection.

But the reading public at large clearly did not share these reservations. "Never perhaps has a book sold so briskly," reported the duc de La Vallière to Voltaire a week after its appearance. People were already going around quoting the phrase "Let us eat Jesuit" as if it were a proverb (D-8072). Doubtless, it was *Candide*'s wit and liveliness that commended it to readers. Such was the view of Voltaire's friend Nicolas Claude Thieriot; those who normally did no more than snicker were laughing openly because it was so enjoyable to read, he told the author (D-8137). Besides, its attack on optimism was not as revolutionary as some of the authoritative reactions might seem to suggest. Leibnizian optimism had never been very popular in France (Madame du Châtelet's enthusiasm for it was a rare exception), and Voltaire cleverly insinuated in various declarations that an attack on this philosophical doctrine was entirely compatible with an orthodox reading of the Bible.

In 1761 Voltaire produced an augmented and definitive edition of *Candide*, the main difference being that chapter 22, on Paris, is extended. The duke of La Vallière, while praising the *conte* on its appearance two years earlier, had indicated that public opinion generally shared his view that this chapter was weak. Voltaire clearly accepted that judgment and made a considerable effort to improve this one section; so much so that chapter 22 is by far the longest in the story. Ironically, its length does little to remedy the original criticism made by the duke, although the chapter contains some interesting passages.

Thereafter, the *conte* was to pass on to posterity unchanged. The dual nature of the critical reception in 1759 would continue. On the one side, *Candide* would inspire a spate of imitations or continuations, at least ten by 1803.[5] But at the same time the work would go on being seen, even right down to our own times, as diabolically comic, the "hideous grin" of an author unfamiliar with the human sentiments of pity and affection.[6] Strange as it may seem to us, the tale did not figure as a prescribed text in French schools until 1968, and even then it was in an abridged version. The alleged "indecencies" were doubtless responsible in large measure. However, since the latter part of the nineteenth century critical opinion has generally come around to the recognition of *Candide* as a masterpiece. Much of the credit for this must go to Gustave Flaubert, who claimed to have read it 100 times, even translating it into English so as to be able to view it in a different light. When a writer of Flaubert's stature could assert that *Candide* was one of only five or six literary models he had looked to, Voltaire's story might be said to have joined at last the inner circle of great classics. Present-day opinion the world over has backed Flaubert's judgment. *Candide* is now available in translations as diverse as Polish, Chinese, and Esperanto, and there is now increasing appreciation for Leonard Bernstein's theatrical adaptation, which, by capturing much of Voltaire's brilliance and vivacity, has become one of the outstanding musicals of our age. In this study we shall try to see why a story rooted so clearly in the eighteenth century can appeal to a public the world over 200 years later.

The *conte* duly received its recognition as a classic in the critical edition by André Morize, which first appeared in 1913. After the "positivist" fashion of the times, this edition is a masterpiece on all the objective aspects of *Candide:* composition, publication, gestation, sources, documentation. Henceforth all serious students of the tale had a reference work that, in many respects, cannot be surpassed. Morize's conclusions about *Candide* sharply rejected the negative, "diabolic" reading of the story: metaphysical speculation may lead only to dupery and disillusionment, but there remains intact a valid sphere of human action and effort. Morize and other Voltaireans did much to rehabilitate the author of *Candide* as a prophet of sane thinking and doing. In this judgment the concluding lines of the story assumed an importance that we should now consider disproportionate, and the controversy over what Candide actually means by his last remark was long-lived. But Morize's overall views, backed by his magisterial erudition, continue to carry authority.

Further new light was not cast on *Candide* until after the Second World War. In 1956 appeared René Pomeau's *La Religion de Voltaire,* which, effectively an intellectual biography, affected our thinking on *Candide* and on every other aspect of the *philosophe's* life and works.[7] Pomeau largely followed Morize's general conclusions but also emphasized the essential importance of style in the success of the *conte.* In addition, Pomeau stressed the irreducible paradox for Voltaire: "God exists, and evil exists." The world has some sort of general order and is not reducible to pure absurdity, for all the horrors. Pomeau's appreciation of this tension underlies much subsequent criticism, among which J. G. Weightman's 1960 article and Jean Sareil's *Essai* (1967) stand out. Each of these carries the argument further, Weightman by underlining the unremitting antithesis between darkness and light, Sareil by laying emphasis on the essentially comic tone.

In the meantime, the meaning of *Candide* was being explored further: by W. H. Barber's useful book in its account of Voltaire and

Leibnizianism (1960), backed up along the same lines by J. H. Brumfitt's edition of *Candide* (1971); by Jean Starobinski on the question of authority (1977); and by Jacques Van den Heuvel on the biographical echoes (1967). An important step forward was achieved when Ira Wade revealed the existence of a hitherto unknown manuscript version of *Candide* (1959), which provided valuable clues on the composition of the *conte*. As the life of Voltaire came to be better known, thanks in large part to Theodore Besterman's editions of the *Correspondence*,[8] *Candide* could be related with more precision to the growing dilemma in Voltaire's mind about the problem of evil.

Sareil, however, had struck an important blow for criticism of *Candide* in arguing that the story has no moral or message. It is above all, he claims, a "liberation."[9] This refreshing approach is a theme of later writings: Jean Starobinski on the fundamental irony of *Candide* (1976); Christiane Mervaud arriving at parallel conclusions from a study of the Venetian episode (1987); and, at greater length, with structuralist overtones of much subtlety and finesse, André Magnan in his edition of *Candide* (1984) and study (1987). A similar path has been pursued—but leading to different conclusions—by Roy Wolper (1969–70) and others. This new reading is challenging enough in its unorthodoxy to merit a separate discussion later.

The numerous editions of *Candide*, popular or scholarly, in French or in translation, have long since ensured universal access to the *conte*. Voltaire, in the contemporary cultural scene, is known above all as its author. It is a sign of the times that Renée Waldinger and others have produced an interesting symposium on how to teach *Candide* (1987). Their collective conclusions indicate how completely, for all its esoteric eighteenth-century resonances, *Candide* is a work that still speaks directly to the problems and inquiries of our own age.

A Reading

❡

4

History

As we shall see, *Candide* has its timeless aspects. But it must equally be said that it also belongs firmly to the world of 1759 and, more broadly, to eighteenth-century Europe. The *conte* is born out of Voltaire's concerns with the world around him. It takes in the Lisbon earthquake of 1755, Robert Damiens's attack upon Louis XV of January 1757, and Admiral Byng's execution of March 1757. Shortly before the English admiral meets his death in *Candide*, the pessimistic Martin has been making the contemptuous point that England and France "are at war for a few acres of snow up Canada way, and spending on this fine war much more than the whole of Canada is worth" (223). The same point was made by Voltaire in a letter of February 1758 in which he expressed his sorrow that people had to "wage a ruinous war" for "a few acres of snow in Acadia" (D-7630). In that same letter he maintained that because of the Seven Years' War people were in a labyrinth from which the only way out was "over dead bodies." Candide will take exactly that way out of the fight between the Abars and the Bulgars: "He traversed heaps of dead and dying" to escape from the Bulgar battlefield (126). Indeed, the famous opening of chapter 3 bears a considerable resemblance to a letter Voltaire had received from the Margravine of Bayreuth describing the battle of Rossbach in November 1757. She wrote later that month: "This [Prussian] army . . . was drawn up in battle order along a line. Then the artillery laid down such a terrible barrage that Frenchmen . . . say

21

each shot killed or wounded eight or nine people. The musketry was no less efficacious. The French were still advancing in columns to attack with the bayonet. . . . The infantry . . . were cut to pieces and totally scattered" (D-7477). This must surely be, at least in part, the origin of Voltaire's account of the fictitious war: "Nothing was as beautiful, as sprightly, as brilliant, as well ordered as the two armies. . . . The guns first of all knocked over approximately six thousand men on each side; next the musketry removed from the best of worlds around nine to ten thousand rascals who were infecting its surface. The bayonet was also the sufficient reason for the death of a few thousand men" (126). The order of detail is the same: the military lineup, the artillery, musketry, bayonet. Voltaire simply transforms an honest account into a display of ironic brilliance. The roles of each weapon are similarly distributed, and the effect of utter devastation is the same. But at Rossbach only the French were routed. It suits Voltaire's strategy to ensure that both sides are shot to pieces in his absurd and horrible battle. The Margravine may also have suggested to Voltaire how to deal with the immediate consequences for Candide when she wrote a few days later to tell him about the starving soldiers who had taken flight and were wandering about Germany like hungry wolves (D-7483). In chapter 3 Candide too flees without direction and runs out of food.

It must not be forgotten that Voltaire was also working on additions to his world history, *Essai sur les moeurs*, in early 1758. In particular, the chapters on the American continent bear close resemblances to *Candide*, showing that they underlie some important parts of the latter work. In chapter 153 of the *Essai* Voltaire deals with the British possessions in colonial America, including Pennsylvania. This colony in particular retained his admiration for being a place of freedom and enlightenment, as it had done ever since he had devoted one of the *Lettres philosophiques* to it 25 years before. In the *Essai sur les moeurs* Voltaire recounts that in Pennsylvania "there are no other dogmas except what was uttered by Penn; so almost everything came down to loving God and human beings; no baptism . . . no priests . . . no judges . . . no doctors."[1] The religion and society of Eldorado are strikingly similar to this: "We do not pray to God . . . we have nothing to ask of him . . . we never stop thanking him" (189). When Candide asks to see some priests he is laughed at; the wise old man he is talking to replies that they are all priests. Besides, religion consists simply of worshiping God. There are no other requirements. Eldoradan society is similarly devoid of courts of justice, since there is no need for litigation or legal judgments; prisons too do not exist. We hear nothing about doctors, probably for the good reason that everyone lives a perfectly healthy life. A further proof that Voltaire has Pennsylvania in mind when describing Eldorado is that the country's currency is the pound sterling (Pennsylvania was still a British colony in 1758). How in literal terms the British coinage came to be applied to a country that had always been sheltered by its mountains from European rapaciousness is left unexplained; it is one of the many fantastic aspects of Eldorado. But the realistic comparisons with an actual colony existing in North America when Voltaire wrote *Candide* must also be borne in mind: Eldorado is, among other things, Quaker country.[2]

The same relationship holds true for chapter 154 of the *Essai sur les moeurs*, which deals with Paraguay. The Jesuit establishment in this Spanish colony is seen as a slave camp where the Jesuits possess all the money; Voltaire notes the ironic paradox that whereas their situation in South America obliges the Jesuits to fight the armies of Spain and Portugal, in Europe the same order acts as confessor to the kings of these two countries. These points are made in even more sardonic form in *Candide* by Cacambo, who has already visited Paraguay: "Los Padres have everything there, and the people nothing; it is the very masterpiece of reason and justice. For my part, I have never seen anything so divine as Los Padres, who wage war here on the King of Spain and the King of Portugal, and in Europe confess these kings. They kill Spaniards here, in Madrid they send them to Heaven. That delights me" (169).

But the most striking example of this concern with the historical present is surely the setting of the opening chapter in Westphalia. The German battlefields of the Seven Years' War provide the ironic location for the Baron's garden, the apparent idyll that turns out on closer examination not to be so. In early 1758 war was raging across Westphalia, as it also was in other parts of Germany. Where better, then, to start this account of "the best of all possible worlds"? Very quickly, the "earthly paradise," as Voltaire sardonically terms it (122), is replaced by a vision of harsh reality.

Candide, impressed into the army of the Bulgar king, finds himself subjected to military discipline, narrowly escapes death for desertion, and becomes an involuntary participant in war against the Abars. The military exercises he undergoes are based on Voltaire's own observations of Frederick's troops during his stay in Berlin. In early 1758—when, it is clear from many references in his letters, he was composing *Candide*—Voltaire remembered how well trained those troops were, how skilled in marching and in battle (D-7565). Candide has undoubtedly become a trained soldier in the military machine that was the Prussian army. It is often overlooked that Candide, far from being a naïve and inexperienced young man wandering the world, is in fact, from the time of his military induction, a highly trained soldier. Indeed, it is the very display of those talents in Cadiz that wins his immediate promotion to infantry company commander (chapter 10).

The German coloring to the story would be emphasized even more in the 1761 editions, when Voltaire extended the title "Candide, or Optimism, translated from the German by Dr. Ralph," by appending, "With the additions found in the Doctor's pocket when he died at Minden in the Year of Grace 1759." Minden, one of the greatest battles of the Seven Years' War, is very suitably a Westphalian town. Later events in 1759, after the first editions of *Candide*, served only to confirm that German province as an admirable choice for the opening scenes.

Westphalia offers one further advantage for Voltaire's story. It was, in 1758, a province, therefore lacking the dignity of a state or a nation. Technically, the little group gathered at the end in the garden is made up mainly of Germans (Candide, Cunégonde, Paquette, Pangloss, and initially the Barón), as well as the Dutchman Martin, the Italians Giroflée and the Old Woman, and the half-caste Cacambo. But it requires a keen analytical sense to remember this. For the main protagonists of *Candide* are wanderers of the world, crossing borders without any sense of exoticism or nostalgia. True, Candide yearns briefly for Westphalia at first; but that is only because he believes Cunégonde is still there, an illusion shattered by Pangloss as early as chapter 4. Thereafter, home for Candide is where Cunégonde may be found. Voltaire's cosmopolitan outlook on the world admits of no nationalist patriotism. He has other concerns. It is entirely fitting that in choosing Westphalia he selects

backwoods territory, already anachronistic at the outset in the alle-
giances to which it clings, and soon to be smashed to pieces beyond
repair. In *Zadig* the hero returns to the Babylon from which he had
set out. In *Candide* that circular possibility is quickly removed.
Candide is doomed to wander until such time as he achieves the
difficult realization that the place where he has come to rest on the
Bosphorus is in fact as much of a home as he will ever know.[3]

But *Candide* is preeminently not a historical novel. Facts about
events like Byng's execution or places like Pennsylvania may be
incorporated, but they will always be surrounded by narrative
fantasy. A simple example is the auto-da-fé, which constitutes one
of the most brilliantly satirical episodes in the whole *conte*. It is
based on historical reality. Auto-da-fés certainly existed in contemporary Portugal, calling down Voltaire's total indictment of the
barbarism that underlay them. He had already attacked this ceremony many times before *Candide*. But the mundane reality of this
particular auto-da-fé is not so convenient for exploitation. There
was apparently none to commemorate the Lisbon earthquake, and
those that took place in ensuing years established no direct
connection, nor was anyone put to death (138, n. 1).

A more complex instance of this historical falsehood occurs in
chapter 26 during the carnival in Venice, when Candide encounters
the six kings. All these kings actually existed, but not at the same
time. The first king, Achmet III, died in 1736, four years before the
second, Ivan VI, was born. The sixth, Theodore, was also dead by
the time *Candide* was being written. Nor was it only death that
prevented some of the kings from being in Venice. Ivan VI was at
this time a prisoner in exile, to be executed in 1764. And the fifth
king would have been unlikely to find himself in the social company
of the fourth. After all, he had driven the latter off the Polish
throne! The situation threatens to become even more improbable
when at the end of the chapter there arrive four further highnesses
who have also lost their states. None of this, however, matters in
literal terms. What we have here is a splendid tableau of dispos-
sessed kings, all of them the victims of war. It is no accident that
they congregate for the carnival. They have the appearance of
player-kings, stage parts devoid of any real meaning or power.
Apart from the brief account by each of the circumstances that led
to his downfall, Voltaire attempts to make no distinction between

them. Their tales contain horrors in the best traditions of *Candide* (none more so than Bonnie Prince Charlie, whose supporters, he recounts, had their hearts torn out, to beat their cheeks with). But otherwise they might be wearing masks, as befits the carnival, hiding all individuality. Here is a demystification of political power, as hollow as a stage crown. Voltaire credits the first five kings with "a noble compassion" (241) as they each give 20 sequins to the impoverished sixth. But the pathos of this act is highlighted when he immediately adds that Candide presented this king with a diamond worth 100 times as much. The kings perform like mechanical puppets, ridiculous figures robbed of all dignity. Such are the perils of official position; dispossession of one's throne means not only loss of power and wealth but reduction to buffoonery. None of their former glory remains to console and uplift them. They are a masquerade of monarchical grandeur, in a way that anticipates Jean Genet's vision of authority during our own times, in plays like *Le Balcon* (1957). Christiane Mervaud has rightly pointed out the structural irony in episodes such as this, suggesting that history, indeed life itself, is one huge carnival, in which folly universally rules the world.[4]

5

Philosophy and Meaning

Candide, as we have seen, sets up optimism for Voltaire's "examination." Why should this particular target have attracted his attention? The answer is contained in Candide's rejoinder to Cacambo, defining optimism. "The mania for asserting that all is well when one is not" (196) points up the unrealistic folly of such a pretense of cheerfulness. But it is not just an absurd belief; important consequences for human behavior flow from it. By acquiescing totally in the way the world is, human beings give up hope, and with it all practical effort. As Voltaire had written in 1756 to a Protestant pastor, "If *all is well*, then all has ever been as it was meant to be." Optimism is therefore a despairing doctrine, "a cruel philosophy under a consoling name." To his pastor friend, Voltaire was able to demonstrate that the biblical "story of the apple" is, humanly speaking, more reasonable, because the Fall, even if it is a myth, at the least implies that a terrible tragedy did occur in Eden, and that it changed God's original plan for humankind (D-6738). But optimism does away with any such concept of a fallen human nature; it simply ignores, in Voltaire's view, the awful realities of evil in the world.

Pangloss, the exponent of optimism, is not just a buffoon. His passive fatalism carries dangerous implications. When Candide attempts to rescue Jacques from drowning, Pangloss restrains him, arguing that "Lisbon harbor was formed expressly for this Anabaptist to drown in it" (134). And drown he does. Unlike so many of the

27

characters reported dead in *Candide,* Jacques dies once and once only; his death is a real event, not a charade. Now, one has to admit that if Candide had tried to save Jacques, he might himself have easily been drowned. But Pangloss does not argue along those lines. He tries to see what is the present situation, then argues that everything in the past has led up to it. Lisbon harbor was created by God for a purpose that would only be fulfilled with Jacques's death. It is teleology run mad. The divine purpose must be sought at every stage, and then one must fit in with it. Pangloss had already made this clear while still in Westphalia: "There is no effect without cause." Everything has its place in the divine plan. "You will note that noses were made to hang spectacles on; therefore we have spectacles. Legs are clearly made to wear breeches, and we have breeches. Stones were created to be carved and made into castles; therefore Milord has a very fine castle: the greatest Baron in the province must have the best home; and as pigs are made to be eaten, we eat pork the whole year round" (119–20). Pangloss's endless chains of arguments always lead to where one is *now.* They give no help for the future, and they take away all initiative. Whether good or bad, things must stay as they are. By contrast, the *real* world is one where things happen, not according to some grand design, but for reasons often malevolent or ridiculous—sometimes both at the same time, as when Pangloss is hanged by the Inquisition for his absurd logic, or even more ludicrous still, Candide is beaten into a pulp for having listened to Pangloss with an approving look on his face. A few years later, Voltaire was to write his *Dictionnaire philosophique* (1764), which includes an article entitled "Chain of Events." In this article Voltaire makes the point that "every effect obviously has its cause . . . but every cause does not have its effect. . . . Everything has fathers, but everything does not always have children."[1] Some actions produce absolutely no difference in the world. If a great king, says Voltaire, sleeps on his left or on his right, spits to his left or his right, it has no bearing upon the effect that the king, however great he is, has upon the world. The "great chain of being" linking everything in the cosmos, which figures so prominently in Pope's *Essay on Man,* simply does not exist. There is no logic or metaphysical finality to the Seven Years' War; yet a brief and terrible succession of causes led to poor old Admiral Byng being shot. If the British government had decided that one must kill an admiral from time to time "to encourage the others," it is an appalling miscarriage of justice. But it certainly was not decided by God on day one of the universe. Voltaire would have wholly approved of the sentiment that "it ain't necessarily so."

It is this inconsequentiality of events that must be borne in mind throughout *Candide*. For a superficial reading of the tale might lead one to believe that, since the optimist Pangloss must be wrong, the pessimist Martin must be right. That reasoning is, of course, very similar to the kinds of argument satirized throughout *Candide*. The hero, horrified by the execution of Byng, immediately asks: "What devil is it that holds sway throughout the world?" (224). But that is how Martin reasons, and by now Candide has fallen under Martin's influence after largely (though not completely) freeing himself from Pangloss's philosophy. At this stage Candide still has a long way to go toward self-liberation, and Martin is a character to be taken much more seriously than Pangloss. He wins the contest set up by Candide to find the most unhappy and embittered man—and there is plenty of competition. Martin has been "robbed by his wife, beaten by his son, and deserted by his daughter" (200); the mean little job he had working for booksellers (one of the professions Voltaire most disliked) has been taken from him; and he has been persecuted by the clergy (another common target) because they thought him a Socinian heretic (chapter 19). If, then, Martin is disenchanted, "it is because I have lived" (229). And he is proved right time and again. He voices the author's bitterness at the corruption of Parisian life (often expressed elsewhere) when he tells Candide that though Parisians laugh all the time, it is while full of rage and complaint or committing the most odious acts (chapter 22). He evokes a terrible picture of Europe at war: "A million murderers in uniform, rushing from one end of Europe to the other, practice murder and pillaging in a disciplined way in order to earn their bread" (202). This figure of one million may at first seem like an exaggeration, but according to René Pomeau, it was probably close to historical reality (202, n. 3). Above all, Martin is adept at sounding out secret unhappiness. In Venice Candide is plunged into deep gloom because there is no sign of Cacambo or of Cunégonde, and so he needs desperately to believe that some happiness still exists in the world. Along comes a young couple, to all appearances deeply happy with each other. Candide imprudently wagers Martin that these two, at least, are content with their lot. But when he has heard their story he has to accept the truth of Martin's rather unkind boast: "Haven't I won the wager outright?" Without doubt, Martin is someone to reckon with.

But the trouble with Martin is that he goes too far. If one million soldiers are laying waste to Europe, the reason, in his view, is simple: "I think that God has abandoned it [the world] to some evil being." As he has just announced, the clergy had persecuted him wrongly for being a Socinian. The fact of the matter is that "I am a Manichean" (201). His Manicheism persuades him that the universe is the home of two warring gods of equal strength, one of good and one of evil, and that it is a struggle neither side will ever win. Furthermore, it is the evil god who has taken possession of our earth. As Martin puts it, "The Devil is so much involved in the affairs of this world that he could well be within my body, just as he is everywhere else" (202). Voltaire himself flirted at times with the Manichean hypothesis of evil; the skeptical Pierre Bayle had taught him the possible advantages of such a philosophy.[2] It had above all the merit of absolving the Lord of Creation from responsibility for evil, which could then be thrust entirely upon the Archenemy of God. But of course, although the Manichean doctrine preserved God's goodness, the sacrifice that had to be made was considerable: God could no longer be considered omnipotent. Voltaire's fascination with Manicheism, however, always stopped short of any real commitment. Intellectually, he found it impossible to square the ordered harmony of the universe obeying regular laws (the constant and fundamental principle of his deist belief) with the notion of two warring deities. Emotionally, he could not accept the postulate that human beings are inherently evil. He always associated Manicheism with the ultimate in pessimism.

This association holds true in *Candide*. For all his penetrating observations on the darker side of life, Martin lacks balance. We are given a firm hint of this almost immediately after he is introduced, when Voltaire tells us that Candide had one great advantage over Martin: he hoped to see Cunégonde again, whereas Martin "had nothing to hope for" (201). Clearly, some irony at Candide's expense underlies this remark, since the naïve quest for Cunégonde always seems likely to end in disillusion. Even so, without hope human beings are but empty shells. Despite his perspicacity, Martin is a walking corpse, with no perspectives on the future. He too, like Pangloss, reasons from things as they are and is useless to anyone seeking help on the most effective method of action. His only advice on how to deal with the troublesome Baron at the end is typically nihilist: throw the Baron into the sea, he suggests. It requires the levelheaded Cacambo to find a practical way out of the dilemma and propose the helpful plan upon which the group decides to act. Like Pangloss, Martin believes in final causes, but in his case they are founded on cosmic pessimism: "Martin above all concluded that man had been born to live out his life amid the convulsions of anxiety or the lethargy of boredom" (256). As a description of Candide's life Martin's conclusion has much to be said for it, especially at this point when, free at last of anxieties, Candide like the others finds himself bored to death. In addition, Pococuranté, without any cause at all for worry in the world, has long since fallen into a hell of apathetic indifference; as we shall see later, boredom (implicit or explicit) plays an important role throughout *Candide*. But life in *Candide* turns out to be more complex than a simple oscillation between ennui and angst.

Not only does Martin place a false emphasis upon the way he generally looks at the world—on occasion he can be downright wrong. When Candide arrives in Venice and finds that Cacambo is not waiting for him as he had promised, our hero falls into a deep depression. Far from consoling him, Martin exploits the occasion for a little sermon: "You really are pretty naïve, to imagine that a half-caste servant, with five or six million in his pockets, will go and seek out your mistress in the back of beyond and bring her to you in Venice. If he finds her, he'll keep her for himself. If he doesn't find her, he'll take another. I advise you to forget your servant Cacambo and your mistress Cunégonde" (225). Voltaire sets up the situation in such a way that, reading it for the first time, one could easily imagine that this will be yet another disappointment for Candide. Indeed, the fact that he says nothing in reply but simply becomes even more gloomy suggests he is acknowledging that Martin is right. Besides, when Cacambo had left Candide back in Surinam, in what seemed like suspect haste, Voltaire's final sentence was ominous: "He was a very good man, this Cacambo" (197). The narrator seems to be taking an ironic distance from his character. Nor is any of this likely to surprise the reader, who has already witnessed such treacheries as the Old Woman being sold into slavery by her fellow Italian.

And then Cacambo actually reappears! So how does Martin react to this totally unexpected demonstration of disinterested loyalty? Does he express surprise, say he regrets having been so dismissive of Cacambo? Not in the least. Whereas Candide is filled with a mixture of joy at seeing Cacambo and pain at learning that Cunégonde is not with him—"his heart agitated, his mind turned upside down"—Martin "looked on at all these adventures impassively" (238). To expect him to do anything else is to assume that he is capable of change; but he is not. Soon after he and Candide first meet, when Martin proclaims his Manicheism, Candide replies: "But there is some good in the world." To which Martin answers, with unusual tact for him but also with total firmness: "That may be . . . but I'm not aware of it" (202).

Because of this stance, he is as inflexible as Pangloss. Voltaire indicates their fundamental likeness in the final chapter when he speaks of Candide "living with the philosopher Pangloss, the philosopher Martin" (254). The latter, just as blinkered as Pangloss, fails to notice the comfort that he still, despite his outlook, derives from life. For he does not appreciate the beneficial effects of companionship. On their Atlantic crossing he and Candide argue constantly, and they get nowhere with each other. This is not, however, a totally futile experience: "But still, they were talking, they were communicating ideas to one another, they were consoling one another" (204). It is yet another instance of philosophy not measuring up to reality. For friendship is one of the positive goods in life. Candide finds solace in Cacambo for a large part of the story, while thinking that only Cunégonde can fulfil his needs. In the final garden he is to discover that, even if sexual love is doomed to end in total disenchantment, the company of his fellow workers is more enduring. This theme of friendship runs through Voltaire's stories as a leitmotiv. In *Zadig*, for instance, the hero's sorrows are assuaged, even in his worst misfortunes, by the loyalty of his servant Cador, and he will himself act as comforter to the wretched fisherman who, like Martin, is betrayed by his wife and is destitute. Voltaire comments authorially: "People say that one is less unhappy when one is not alone; . . . that is not out of malice, but of need. One feels drawn toward an unfortunate as to one's fellow. The joy of a happy man would be an insult; but two unhappy people are like two delicate shrubs that, leaning on one another, fortify each other against the storm" (Deloffre and Van den Heuvel, 96 –97). Like Vladimir and Estragon in Samuel Beckett's *Waiting for Godot* (1952), friendship is a support, however limited, against harsh existence. Voltaire's characters are naturally gregarious. For them, the most wretched state of all is one of total isolation. It is significant for the tone of the *conte* that no one, not even Candide, is left on his own for the space of a whole chapter.

As Candide and Martin near the end of their journey across the Atlantic, Candide asks a question that incorporates his feelings of despair at that moment about the human race:

> "Do you think," said Candide, "that men have always massacred each other as they do today? that they have always been liars, cheats, treacherous, ingrates, brigands, weak, flighty, cowards, envious, greedy, drunkards, misers, ambitious, bloodthirsty, slanderers, debauched, fanatics, hypocrites, and fools?" "Do you think," said Martin, "that sparrow hawks have always eaten pigeons when they have discovered them?" "Yes, probably," said Candide. "Well then," said Martin, "if sparrow hawks have always had the same disposition, why do you expect men to have changed theirs?" "Oh," said Candide, "there's a great deal of difference, for free will . . ." While debating thus, they arrived at Bordeaux. (207)

This extraordinary outburst by Candide follows closely on the particularly painful experiences he suffers in Surinam at the hands of the rascally merchant Vanderdendur and subsequently in the law courts. This is undoubtedly one of his moments of greatest dejection in the whole *conte*, when "human wickedness revealed itself to his mind in all its ugliness" (199). It is in direct consequence of this despair that he organizes the contest to find the unhappiest man, which will eventually bring Martin into his life. Even so, he clings illogically to some vague notion of free will, as we can see. But it is Martin's more trenchant observations that concern us directly at this point. For in his opinion there has never been anything in human nature except the inclinations to slaughter and deceit. Such a total view runs into difficulties once it encounters a rare type of human being like Cacambo or Jacques the Anabaptist.

Jacques's own qualities will be considered later. For the moment, let us note his philosophy of human nature, so radically different from Martin's. On the way to Lisbon he tells Pangloss that he cannot share the latter's optimism: "Men . . . must have corrupted Nature a little, for they were not born wolves, and they have become wolves. God did not give them heavy cannon or bayonets; and they have manufactured themselves bayonets and cannon to destroy each other" (132). This is a sort of halfway point between the unsubtle conclusions of both Pangloss and Martin, as befits the noblest character in *Candide*. It sounds very like the picture painted by Jean-Jacques Rousseau in his *Discours sur l'origine de l'inégalité* (1755), which Voltaire had read, appending marginal comments on his own copy.

But to conclude that Voltaire is thereby taking a simple Rousseauist view of the world would be folly indeed. For it is Pangloss who holds to one of Rousseau's most basic tenets in the *Discours* when he opines that "the riches of the earth are common to all men" and that "each person has an equal right to them" (150). When Rousseau took the selfsame approach at the beginning of the second part of the *Discours*, Voltaire had commented witheringly: "That is the philosophy of a beggar who would like the rich to be robbed by the poor."[3] In brief, nothing in Jacques's utterance or in any other part of *Candide* suggests that Voltaire is settling for a philosophically systematic view of human nature, its origins, and its significance.

For *Candide* is not, in reality, a philosophical novel. Voltaire was not out to make a coherent general statement about man's place in the world. He had a different purpose in *Candide*.

Now, this may at first sound like heresy. Do we not refer commonly to Voltaire's stories, and preeminently *Candide*, as *contes philosophiques*? Is not Voltaire here attacking a philosophical concept? Do not such metaphysical terms as "sufficient reason" and "Manicheism" get bandied about?

All this is true—though it should be added that Voltaire did not use the term "philosophical tale" until a good deal later, and that in any case *philosophie* held a much wider meaning in eighteenth-century France than it does nowadays. Philosophy was not only concerned with metaphysics, ontology, and logic but also with how a human being should act in the world and toward his fellowmen.

In that less rigorous sense, *Candide* easily qualifies. This may, however, be considered just a technical argument about the meaning of the term *philosophy* 200 years ago. We must address the question on a wider front.

To be sure, we are told that Martin is a Manichean. But we do not need to know a great deal about Manicheism in order to understand him. His philosophy is essentially a belief that the Devil rules the world—not a very sophisticated concept. It is also true that Pangloss, in the early pages of the story, informs us that things exist necessarily for the best possible end. But that too can hardly count as high-flown philosophy, and as we have seen, Pangloss very quickly brings teleological reasoning down to an argument for eating pork all year round. Worse is to follow. For Pangloss's lesson of "experimental physics" to the chambermaid allows Cunégonde an excellent opportunity for observation, in which "she saw clearly the sufficient reason of the doctor, its effects and causes" (120). Such is the treatment generally meted out to philosophical discourse in *Candide*. Things tend to be quickly reduced to an earthy level. When poor Candide, destitute and starving, arrives in Holland, he trots out the Panglossian line that there is no effect without cause, while indicating at the same time that what really matters is that he is in desperate need of food. Once more, philosophy carries with it more than purely abstract consequences. Since Candide cannot dogmatically assert that the Pope is the Antichrist, it is his fate to have a bucket filled with unspeakable contents poured over his head. Furthermore, when Pangloss vanishes from the scene in chapter 6, not to reappear until three chapters from the end, the jargon disappears with him. The only connecting "philosophical" thread is Candide's oscillating opinion about whether Westphalia is the best of all possible worlds; here again, we are hardly called upon to reflect deeply. By the time Pangloss reappears Martin is already ensconced as Candide's companion. Surely, if *Candide* were truly a "philosophical novel" this would be the ideal opportunity for a thoroughgoing debate about the world. Well, that debate takes place—but offstage, so to speak. In the penultimate chapter, Voltaire tells us not only that they reason together but that Candide, the Baron, and Cacambo all join in, arguing "about the contingent or noncontingent events of this universe . . . effects and causes, moral and physical evil, liberty, and necessity" (252).

However, we never hear another word about the nature of those arguments. They are merely a way of passing the time until the group arrives at the place where Cunégonde and the Old Woman are slaves. Philosophy, like storytelling, can serve to fill up empty hours. Indeed, the five men have not only been disputing about great ideas, they have also been recounting their adventures, so that as well as contingency, evil, and necessity, their debates address "the consolations one can enjoy when on the Turkish galleys" (252). These points immediately succeed one another in Voltaire's text; philosophical inquiry of the metaphysical kind has no higher value, evidently, than the purely anecdotal.

In this sort of way the tone of *Candide* is completely different from that of the *Poème sur le désastre de Lisbonne,* which in some respects has always been regarded as the verse forerunner of the *conte.* The poem about the Lisbon earthquake is undoubtedly philosophical in nature and, as we have seen, full of anguished questioning. There is not a hint of humor anywhere in it. If it can be said to contain irony, that irony is of an unambiguously tragic kind, as, for instance, in the trenchant description of the universal round of slaughter. The basic underlying question of the Lisbon poem is, Why? In keeping with that, the expression is often simply interrogative. Four direct questions occur in the first 20 verses, and no fewer than 20 altogether in the entire work. This interrogation rises to a climactic line near the end, where everything about the human condition is placed in doubt: "What am I, where am I, whither am I going, and whence do I come?"[4] In the face of such uncertainty, it is hardly to be wondered at that Voltaire concludes the poem by rejecting every positive attempt to explain the universe: not only the explanations of Leibniz and Pope and of orthodox Catholicism, but even those of Plato and Epicurus. Ultimately, he places his trust in only one thinker, the skeptic Pierre Bayle. For Bayle, says Voltaire, teaches one to doubt, and that can be the only sensible approach, since all absolute knowledge is kept hidden from us: "The book of Fate is closed to our gaze" (477). We must practice doubt, but we may also be permitted to hope—the one gleam of light in an otherwise dark universe and on which the poem concludes.

By the time of *Candide* three years later, Voltaire had, as it were, absorbed into himself the lessons of the *Poème sur Lisbonne.*

Philosophical optimism is still as much of a cruel joke played upon the human race, but there no longer seems any point in going on about suffering as though it were a surprising new experience. The Old Woman has seen and undergone the worst atrocities of anyone in the story. But she feels no particular sense of horror in telling them over. Indeed, as she points out, she is recounting her tale simply because Cunégonde was foolish enough to think that no one had suffered as she had. She concludes her dreadful story with these words to Cunégonde: "I would never even have spoken of my misfortunes if you hadn't irritated me slightly and if it were not customary on a ship to tell stories to avoid boredom" (163). It is a marvelous throwaway line. The Old Woman wants to put Cunégonde right, but she also tells stories to pass the time. Here again, *Candide* anticipates Beckett's *Godot.*

When, therefore, the Old Woman has some particularly awful detail to tell, she slides over it as though it were of no importance. She had in her youth been betrothed to a handsome prince who loved her. But at the wedding feast a jealous ex-mistress served him chocolate, and in less than two hours he died "in terrible convulsions." Lest our sympathies become engaged, she immediately adds, "But it's of no consequence whatsoever" (154). So it will always be for her thereafter. After an appalling massacre that she alone survives, she recovers consciousness to find a handsome young man moving about on top of her. His motives are obvious and undisguised, for he gives eloquent voice to a lament that he was castrated when still a schoolboy. This mournful cry, in Italian,[5] informs her that he is her compatriot; indeed, it turns out that he was her music teacher when she was a child. Will this turn out happily? We should have been warned by his attempt to abuse her body as she lay defenseless. Despite his initial offer of help to her in her desperate state, the same lack of humanity surfaces as soon as they leave Morocco: instead of taking her back to Italy as he had promised, he simply sells her into slavery in Algiers. It is a particularly base act of treachery. But the Old Woman makes no comment on it. Such is the world. Like Martin, she has lived—"I am experienced, I know the world"—and she anticipates Martin in claiming that whomever you ask to tell you his story will confess that he has often cursed his life and told himself that he is the most wretched of men. But unlike Martin, she is no philosopher. She has no system of reasoning to explain the world. When need be she acts, like Cacambo, in practical and unsentimental ways. If Candide has to be jettisoned in Buenos Aires because the murders he committed in Lisbon have been traced to him, so be it. It is the only way she can save her mistress—and also, of course, her own skin.

While the Old Woman is far too pragmatic to waste time on philosophy, she has developed a view of human nature out of her multiple experiences. She has known misery and humiliation, folly, degradation. A hundred times over she has wanted to kill herself, she says. But always the instinct to go on living has been paramount. For the majority of people, suicide is simply not an answer. In all her wanderings among wretched and oppressed people she has known only 12 who put an end to their misery: three blacks, four Englishmen, four Genevans, and a German professor. All these except for the blacks (we shall shortly look at Voltaire's treatment of the black slave) are noted with a certain amount of ironic detachment. The English were, in the eighteenth century, considered the suicidal nation par excellence. (Voltaire once propounded the thesis that it was caused by the east wind.) The Genevans, as we have noticed, were no longer very popular with the *philosophe* after three years' living in their midst. The suicide of the German professor is a reference to one Robeck, a real person who had drowned himself in 1739. But the anticlimactic effect of "a German professor named Robeck" at the end of the list is surely not meant to qualify as tragedy or even pathos. (Pangloss, it may be recalled, is in despair near the end of *Candide* because he never made his name in a German university; such buffoon aspirations set the unfortunate Robeck in his proper context.) One may say, then, that apart from blacks (who were probably condemned to be slaves), suicide is an option only for foolish eccentrics. For your average white European, life is for living, despite all its drawbacks.

Now, it is very tempting to read this in a complacent light. In the twentieth century Camus was to suggest in *The Myth of Sisyphus* (1942) that the only question of any real significance is, Is life worth living? His answer, too, is an affirmative one: man must "revolt" against his fate, in the name of justice and happiness.[6] But Voltaire's view, as expressed through the Old Woman, is a good deal more somber and ironic than that. In her opinion, life is, for most people, an unhappy experience. Through the Old Woman, as again later through Martin, Voltaire stresses the point that cheerfulness is usually a mask that people put on. Yet despite these discouragements people want to go on surviving. She describes this impulse in piquant terms that not even the "sublime misanthrope" Blaise Pascal (Voltaire's phrase for him) could have bettered: "This ridiculous weakness is perhaps one of our most desolating instincts; for is anything more foolish than to want to carry around unceasingly a burden that one wants to cast on the ground? to hate oneself, and to cling to one's existence? in brief, to caress the serpent that devours us, until he has eaten our heart out?" (162).

One is reminded of Hamlet's famous soliloquy "To be or not to be," which impressed Voltaire early in his stay in England; he referred to it only a few months after his arrival in 1726, when writing about his sister's death. Later, he would include his translation of the speech in the *Lettres philosophiques*. But the comparison serves only to point up the contrast. For Hamlet's soliloquy is in keeping with high tragedy. Life is full of calamity, such that every true man would put an end to it. But, for Hamlet, "the dread of something after death" stays our hand. In *Candide*, by contrast, the consideration of an afterlife does not enter into it. It is simply our ridiculous life force that keeps us going. Unlike Hamlet, the characters in *Candide* do not contemplate death. It is as though the self-preservation instinct acts all on its own, quite independent of any rationality of judgment. The Old Woman is right to define it as a ridiculous weakness. There is an element of the absurdly comic about it. No one exemplifies it better than our naïve hero. He is saved from the auto-da-fé by the Old Woman, but he is in a dreadful physical and mental state: all bloody from his beating, scarcely able to stand up, but also deep in despair at having lost Pangloss and also from the news (later to prove false) that Pangloss had brought of Cunégonde's death. But the Old Woman, practical as ever, gives him a pot of ointment and says to him, "Rub yourself with ointment, eat and sleep." And Candide, "despite so many misfortunes, ate and slept" (141). It is truly amazing what a little ointment can do for someone. In two days he is able to walk a quarter of a mile to where Cunégonde is in hiding. After their marvelous reconciliation, of course there can be no doubt that he will soon be fully restored to health.

Another excellent example of this mechanical reflex occurs later, when Candide and Cacambo are obliged to flee from the Jesuit settlement in Paraguay after Candide, as they think, has killed Cunégonde's brother. Cacambo displays the same quick-wittedness on behalf of his master as the Old Woman had done for her mistress, and he extricates Candide in the twinkling of an eye, as Voltaire puts it. Once they have made a clean escape, Cacambo suggests that they have something to eat. Candide rounds on him indignantly: "How can you want me to me eat ham, when I have killed the Baron's son and see myself doomed never to look again upon the fair Cunégonde for the rest of my days? What avails it to me to prolong my wretched life, since I must drag it out far from her in remorse and despair?" But, as Voltaire tells us, Cacambo has already begun eating, unaffected by such tragic utterances. There is nothing more infectious for a healthy man who is hungry than the sight of a companion eating. Candide is won over, despite himself, and without realizing it: "While speaking thus, he could not refrain from eating" (176). Disasters notwithstanding, banal life goes on regardless, as though nature were taking care of itself without reference to the higher and more complex feelings of the human race.

To my mind, it is the Old Woman, in the passage about suicide quoted above, who comes closest of all the characters to articulating the special quality of *Candide*. Many are the critics who have spoken of Voltaire's satanism, of his delight in the horrible.[7] That element is undeniably present. But to dwell exclusively upon the savagery of the satire would be to limit the resonance of *Candide* very seriously. Perhaps no one has summed up the distinctive tone of the *conte* better than J. G. Weightman: "In this one book, the horror of evil and an instinctive zest for life are almost equally matched and it is the contrast between them . . . which produces the unique tragi-comic vibration . . . an unappeasable sense of the mystery and horror of life is accompanied, at every step, by an instinctive animal resilience. . . . *Candide* throbs from end to end with a paradoxical quality which might be described as a despairing hope or a relentless charity."[8] As Weightman stresses, there is a deeply inherent duality in Voltaire's vision of the world. Although the proportions may be far from equal, there is no good without evil, no evil without good. Human beings may not often be happy, or for very long, it is true. But it is equally the case that human beings have within them the capacity for happiness. So, in Voltaire's *contes,* there is an incessant oscillation. The laughter is ephemeral, but in most cases (the black slave always being an exception) so too are the tears. Life moves on again after the drowning, after the auto-da-fé, after the rape or the murder. The survivors . . . survive. The world will never make rational sense. But life carries on. As Voltaire had already put it in a much earlier work, if there is constant destruction in the cosmic economy, there is also constant regeneration.[9] A Voltaire *conte* published a decade after *Candide, La Princesse de Babylone* (1768), stresses the universality of resurrection in this world. Grubs reemerge as butterflies; a walnut placed in the earth is reborn as a walnut tree; animal corpses interred in the ground feed other animals, of which they become a part (Deloffre and Van den Heuvel, 373). Like slaughter, rebirth is also continual and also universal.

Here seems to me to reside the essential Voltairean worldview, which the author perhaps only in *Candide* interprets with complete persuasiveness in his fiction. At other times he falls too easily into the sentimental or the didactic mode. Indeed, even in this tale the balance is precarious, as in chapter 22 on Paris, generally held to be the weakest in the whole book. More closely related, however, to the problem of evil is the episode of the black slave (chapter 19).

We know that this episode was added very late in the composition of *Candide,* for it does not figure in the La Vallière manuscript. That version, the only manuscript copy we have of the work (apart from some later corrections to chapter 22), was sent to the duc de La Vallière in the autumn of 1758 and probably dates from October of that year (47), three months before the *conte* was dispatched for publication. At this stage, although the whole tale substantially existed already in its first published version, the black slave did not appear. The second and third paragraphs of chapter 19 were simply inserted subsequently. Late in 1758 Voltaire clearly felt the need to incorporate into his encyclopedic view of the world a striking illustration of the effects of colonial slavery. (There are, of course, numerous instances of servitude elsewhere in *Candide:* the hero is press-ganged into the Bulgar army, and the three main female characters, Cunégonde, the Old Woman, and Paquette, all offer evidence of how often woman's condition can be one of enslavement.) What had occurred to remind Voltaire of this omission? His inspiration very probably came from reading a work by a fellow *philosophe,* Claude Helvétius, entitled *De l'esprit* (1758), which Voltaire had received in mid-October. Helvétius discusses the slave trade, including the poignant comment: "It will be a matter of common agreement that not a barrel of sugar arrives in Europe which is not stained with human blood. So, what man seeing the miseries caused by the cultivation and export of this commodity would refuse to give it up and not sacrifice a pleasure bought with the tears and deaths of so many wretched people? Let us avert our glance from a sight so appalling, which inflicts so much shame and horror upon the human race" (cited in Pomeau, 46). Here, surely, we have the inspiration for one of the most trenchant sentences in *Candide:* "It's at this price that you eat sugar in Europe" (195–96).

If the link with Helvétius is accepted, Voltaire would have inserted this new episode somewhere between the end of October and about the middle of December, his heart obviously stirred by the plight of the slaves. (A similar concern is shown in chapter 152 of his historical work, the *Essai sur les moeurs,* which he was also writing at this time.) He evokes the miserable existence of a people who received only two items of clothing a year, who were sentenced to having a leg mutilated if they tried to escape, and whose arm was cut off if their fingers were caught in the mill; all these conditions were legally in force at the time (Pomeau, 195, n. 4).

But one has to ask whether this awful spectacle, for all its eloquence, fits in completely with the rest of the work. This is the place in the text where Candide gives his succinct definition of optimism (196). But are we witnessing the same Candide as elsewhere? For here we find him bursting out in indignation, in a manner unparalleled anywhere else in the story. It does not greatly matter if he announces, as he does, that he is at last renouncing optimism, for he had already registered strong doubts about it after the Old Woman's tale (chapter 13), and about Pangloss's teaching once he had seen Eldorado (chapter 18). But it is the way he acts as spokesman for Voltaire that is unexpected and somewhat disconcerting. For throughout the *conte,* right up to the very final paragraphs, the hero is consistently viewed with a certain ironic detachment. Even at the end he is saying no more than that "we must cultivate our garden" (260). By contrast, here is the unique instance where Candide openly denounces optimism.

One may hazard the speculation that in this late addition to the *conte* we are seeing the first evidence of the later Voltaire, the Voltaire who would crusade ceaselessly until the end of his life in the cause of justice and who would enlist the aid of trenchant propaganda for his purpose. This Voltaire can already be seen in his correspondence of the final weeks of 1758, and the reason for the new emphasis seems clear: he had discovered the reality of social conditions at Ferney, where he would the following year become the owner and seigneur. On these lands lived, he wrote on 18 November, "unfortunates who hardly have the wherewithal to eat a little black bread." Half the tenants were dying of poverty, the other half were in jail on ridiculous charges. "My heart is torn when I witness so many miseries. I am buying Ferney just to do some good there" (D-7946). The editor Theodore Besterman comments that "no such language as this is to be found in any previous writing by Voltaire. . . . It is as if the condition of the peasants and the land had caused all his thinking suddenly to come to a point, exploding in this trumpet-call of social protest" (D-7946, Commentary). This too is the language of the black slave episode. By having the slave explicitly point out, "It's at this price that you eat sugar in Europe," the author is clearly aiming to subvert his reader's complacency and give him a bad conscience. The reader is forced into direct confrontation and the ground is taken away from under his feet, in a style reminiscent of Jonathan Swift's in *Gulliver's Travels* (1726)—which Voltaire, incidentally, had read and admired when the novel appeared during his stay in England.

But the satiric approach of the tale as a whole is more direct and subtle than that. The tone here, by contrast, is sharply emotional and belongs more to a later *conte* like *L'Ingénu* (1767) than to *Candide*. Besides, another problem occurs. Within the plot of the story, what is to be done about the black slave? In short, plainly nothing. Candide "wept tears as he looked at his black companion; and weeping, he went into Surinam" (196). What else could he possibly have done for this poor mutilated wretch? Colonial slavery was beyond Voltaire's powers of intervention; like Candide, an individual, even a polemicist of Voltaire's stature could only express outrage. No viable answer was possible for black slaves in Candide's Turkish garden. Impotent sorrow is all that the hero can register in the face of a problem beyond his capacity to affect. And impotent sorrow was not Voltaire's way. He preferred taking practical initiatives that were within his power. Similarly, Candide *could* save Paquette and Giroflée from poverty, he *could* rescue Pangloss from the galleys and Cunégonde and the Old Woman from domestic slavery. And he did.

The episode concerning the black slave, therefore, constitutes a paradox. It has the capacity to affect the reader deeply as an isolated incident, but within its context it is an interpolation at odds with the surrounding text. The general view taken of the world in *Candide* is that it affords material for a huge cosmic joke on the human race; people rush around crazily or preen themselves self-importantly in a universe where evil and, in a much lesser degree, good exist without rhyme or reason. It is in this light that we should now consider the final scenes and the famous last words, "we must cultivate our garden," over which so much ink has been spilled. Is the final remark meant as a call to social action, a fore-runner of the crusading Voltaire of later years? Or is the ending intended to suggest a kind of fatalistic inaction, a defensive self-protection in which the little group shuts out all concern with outside society?

It seems to me that neither of these positions is defensible. We have just seen how the didactic approach shown in the treatment of the colonial slave jars with the overall register of *Candide*. There is a consistent relationship, it is true, between the satiric tone of the *conte* and Voltaire's calls to action later in his life; the underlying attitudes are essentially the same. But the Voltaire of early and mid-1758 was not yet devoting all his energies to protest. Admiral Byng's execution was a case of official madness run riot, "in order to encourage the others." It is quite a different stance from that which Voltaire would take in 1762 to rehabilitate Jean Calas's reputation after the miscarriage of justice in Toulouse. Both Byng and Calas were dead because of the folly of so-called legal justice. Voltaire, it is true, had tried to intervene on Byng's behalf, without success. But by the time of *Candide* that was long since a lost cause, the occasion only for mordant sardonicism. Whereas Calas would become a crusade enlisting all his direct, dynamic energies in order to right a wrong.

In parallel fashion, the view that at the end Candide and his companions have resigned themselves to an inward-looking passivity goes against everything else Voltaire ever urged. "Man was born for action, as fire flares upwards and stones fall to the ground," he had written in the *Lettres philosophiques* (2:205-6). The human necessity to be active was, he believed, as much of a natural law as the force of fire or of gravitation. Such action, too, needed to be productively meaningful, not just a way of killing time. It is no accident that the group finishes up not in a castle or a city but in a garden, at work that will yield produce and enhance the quality of life. The *conte* has made a ceaseless onslaught upon optimism, which Voltaire had also repeatedly denounced in his correspondence because it destroyed the will to initiative. It would therefore be strange to conclude that at the end of the story Candide has, in a topsy-turvy way, joined forces with the optimists.

That viewpoint has, however, been given a new airing in a radically revisionist thesis by Roy Wolper. Wolper's reading of *Candide* proposes that, indeed, absolutely nothing has changed at the end—because Candide remains a total fool right up to the last word of the story. He contends that the hero has done no more than fulfill his earliest dreams: to be born the Baron Thunder-ten-tronckh, to see Cunégonde every day, and to listen to Pangloss (chapter 1). Candide, writes Wolper, is now "a surrogate baron . . . married to Lady Cunégonde . . . and has Pangloss as a constant conversationalist."[10] He has achieved nothing, he is still an ironic hero. The final solution, that work cures boredom, vice, and need, is irrelevant to the sufferings we have been witnessing and the abuses and persecution practiced on all sides. By clinging to the belief in work, "the little group itself *contributes* to the ongoing cruelty and carnage: the produce from the garden will nourish the Vanderdendurs, the Gauchats, the Dutch magistrates, the Christian prelates" (Wolper, 273). At the end Candide, it is true, is no longer Pangloss's puppet; but that is merely because he has found a new puppeteer in the Old Turk, the former whose advice he now slavishly follows as he had previously followed Pangloss's. He has learned little about virtue and helping others. Jacques's example has been unavailing. The values of *Candide* are not Candide's. "At the end, Candide, reduced to petty revenge, sells Cunégonde's brother into a galley" (Wolper, 277).

This is a refreshingly provocative point of view that has the great merit of forcing critics of *Candide* to think again about the basic meaning of the story. And it has won admirers, the more so as Professor Wolper has gone on extending his reappraisals to one Voltaire story after another.[11] But the danger is that he risks throwing out the baby with the bathwater. His contention is that the banality of the ending in no way does justice to the horrors of man's inhumanity to man that have been described earlier. The force of this argument merits serious discussion. But should one not, first of all, put the question back to Wolper: What significance can *Candide* hold if the ending is an empty shell? If, after every terrible experience the reader has been through, the end merely shows us an unteachable marionette, one has to ask, Why bother? What is the point of it all? To which questions Professor Wolper has already given his reply: there *are* values—social concern and education—and these are enshrined in "the spirit Jacques has" (Wolper, 277). In other words, there *is* a hero to *Candide*. Unfortunately, that hero appears for only just over one chapter of the 30 (to be more precise, 134 lines out of more than 3,000 in the Pomeau edition) and is very little heard of again in the rest of the story. This is no Banquo's ghost to haunt Macbeth, no Julius Caesar living on after death to trouble Brutus and Cassius. We shall consider in a later chapter the qualities in Jacques's character; they are unique in the *conte*. But they are never given a chance to dominate, for the tale is not essentially about those qualities, which inevitably meet with a quick end in the world of *Candide*.

The Wolper view, by seeking to demean the significance of Candide's position at the end, aims to destroy the validity of the ending as a way forward. Not only has Candide learned nothing; he is stupid to the point of brutality. The hero's reaction to Cunégonde's brother, cited above, is a case in point: Candide, in selling the Baron back to the galleys, is "reduced to petty revenge." But, in fact, in the story it is not like that. First of all, if the Baron had stayed with the group, there would have been an irreducible conflict. For Cunégonde has already reminded Candide of his earlier promise to marry her, "in a manner so peremptory that Candide did not dare to refuse her" (253). When the Baron, however, objects, because of the eternal shame it would bring upon the family in the ranks of the German nobility, Cunégonde throws herself at his feet. But to no avail; "he was inflexible" (253). This paradoxical situation exasperates Candide almost beyond endurance. He no longer pretends complicity with Cunégonde's delusion that she has kept her beautiful looks: "You utter fool," Candide says to the Baron, "I rescued you from the galleys, paid your ransom, also paid your sister's; she was scouring dishes here, she is ugly, I have the decency to make her my wife, and you still intend to oppose it; I should kill you again if I were to give vent to my anger" (253). But, as Voltaire goes on to show in the following sentences, he contains his anger. As a man of honor, he cannot go back on his word, especially under Cunégonde's relentless pressure. Besides, the Baron's infuriating impudence is a powerful incentive in itself to press on with the marriage. So Cunégonde's brother will have to go; no other solution is possible. Candide acts not out of revenge but out of self-respect reinforced by practical common sense. That much decided, the question then remains: What is to be done with the Baron? We have already noted that the intemperate solution comes, not from Candide, but from Martin, who simply wants to throw him into the sea. Candide, for his part, decides nothing. He has consulted Pangloss, Martin, and Cacambo; only Cacambo produces a helpful answer. It is, moreover, a highly constructive piece of advice. For the Baron is returned to the galleys only as a provisional step, "after which he would be sent to Rome to the Father-General by the first vessel" (254). In short, he will be returned to the authorities who recruited him for Paraguay in the first place. Some hope may still be held out of a new career for him. He has shown himself beyond saving within the little community in the Turkish garden, but so far as his impossible snobbishness will ever permit it, he may yet make something of himself. Cacambo's bright idea is, we are told, generally approved, including by the sagacious Old Woman. Only Cunégonde is not let in on the decision, for obvious reasons.

It is worth going into this much detail on a single point affecting the final outcome in the *conte* because it shows how, by careful reading of the text, a dismissive judgment on the hero cannot be sustained. Indeed, when we come to consider Candide's role in the tale, we shall see how much Voltaire allows him to develop. For the moment, let us also note that, in the final chapter, the hero is no "surrogate Baron" (Wolper, 268). The original Baron of chapter 1 lived, in tranquil condescension, a life of utter falsity. On occasion, his farmyard dogs were a makeshift hunting pack and his stable boys became huntsmen. The village curate was deemed to be his "Grand Almoner," and everyone dutifully laughed at his stories. Benevolent though this arrangement may at first appear to be, its underpinning is a rigid philosophical and social order based on keeping things exactly as they are. That is why Pangloss's optimism, with its assurance that this life cannot be bettered, fits in so admirably. But when Candide strays, however briefly, from the deferential position he is expected to maintain in the household, he is literally booted out by the Baron without further ado.

Nothing of this feudal hierarchy remains in the final episode. Everyone contributes on an equal footing; no one is treated as an inferior. There is no underlying religious principle and no representative of the clergy (except a renegade monk). The community defers to nobody; it is entirely made up of commoners. Unlike Candide's expulsion from the castle of Thunder-ten-tronckh, a brutally authoritarian act by the Baron, the expulsion of Cunégonde's brother is decided on after general discussion. There are, indeed, parallels to be drawn between the first and the last chapters of *Candide*. But the superficial comparisons serve only to heighten the fundamental contrasts.[12]

The basic contention of the Wolper school is that the ending of *Candide* is a deliberately derisory anticlimax on Voltaire's part. This opinion is well summed up by Theodore Braun in a strong defense of Wolper's position. He argues that the Old Turk's famous advice ("Work keeps away from us three great evils, boredom, vice and need") is quite invalid in view of what has gone before: "Rape, murder, plunder, assassination, the slaughter of innocents, kidnappings, massacres occur everywhere, in Europe, in Africa, in the Middle East, in the New World. Workers like the Negro slave are mutilated; others who work (judges, law clerks, businessmen) are rapacious thieves; productive workers are often poor and hungry or ill-fed, while those who exploit their labours are rich and satisfied (e.g., the Paraguayan Indians and the Jesuits); even the garden group itself cannot escape boredom through work" (Braun, 314). It is a powerful statement, taking in as it does a horrendous collective picture of the world as we have seen it in *Candide*.

Here too, however, one must guard against approximations. The little group, it is true, has to face the problem of boredom. But this is only at the beginning of the last chapter. They are bored, in fact, because they are *not* working, except for Cacambo, who in consequence has too much to do and curses his situation. At this point, the members are for the most part spending their time in argument, either on "metaphysics and morality" or on the melancholy spectacle of those in authority in Constantinople being constantly replaced and banished into exile. It is this repetitive, unproductive round (even Cacambo's gardening is a depressing chore) that provokes their terrible boredom. Only the pessimistic Martin "accepted things with patience" (255). But then, he would, wouldn't he? For the moment, everything is conveniently bearing out his philosophy that nothing can be improved. By contrast, when at last the group accepts the Old Turk's advice, boredom simply disappears. In brief, they *do* escape boredom through work.

This again is a detail that helps to illuminate the general picture. For the main thrust of the Braun-Wolper thesis is larger: that the banal recipe of work is not a suitable response to the world's atrocities. To answer this, one must consider the Old Turk's remark in its context and on its merits. His life is not heroic. He does not go looking for noble causes. He assumes that political careers sometimes lead to misery, and that the misery is probably deserved. In the meantime, he has created a quiet haven of contentment, and that is enough for him. All he knows is that work keeps certain large wolves from the door. The first, given pride of place, is boredom.

This can hardly be accounted an accident. The Old Woman, in the final chapter, asks whether all the terrible atrocities she and the others have suffered—the multiple rapes, the excised buttock, Candide's running the gauntlet of the regiment, Pangloss's hanging, and so on—were actually worse than "being here doing nothing" (255–56). Candide acknowledges that it is a good question and does not attempt to answer it. Terrible as actual suffering is, ennui may well be more terrible yet, for it destroys the soul. The supreme instance in *Candide* is Pococuranté, whom we shall consider later. But he is not alone in his apprehensions. Martin latches onto the Old Woman's remark in order to suggest, characteristically, that man is doomed to live in the convulsions of anxiety or the lethargy of boredom. But earlier on in the *conte* risks of tedium have been faced and indeed overcome. The need to escape from being bored is one of the two reasons the Old Woman gives for telling her story during the Atlantic voyage. The return journey is also filled up with talk, endless philosophical disputes between Martin and Candide that achieve nothing except the consolation of communicating with a fellow being. By contrast, Paris, for instance, is a place of non-communication. The gambling at the house of the marquise de Parolignac is a wretched charade, marked by silences, suspicion, and constant cheating. The supper that follows is no better; initial silence is succeeded by a rush of talk, but it is a meaningless jumble of poor jokes, false rumors, bad arguments, and a lot of backbiting. The evening provides yet another example of the essential vacuity beneath the glittering surface once life has been reduced to a meaningless social round.

So the lethal quality of languor is accorded pride of place in the Turkish farmer's summation, along the lines of what has gone before in the *conte*. Thereafter come vice and need—the one so often, in *Candide*, dependent on the other, as Paquette, for example, would readily confirm. But these two little words must be taken at their full value. What we have been experiencing throughout the tale is the combined effect of vicious behavior (murder, rape, plunder, treachery) and need (the black slave, the poor Indians, even Candide himself before he reaches Eldorado). The Old Turk, though he may have no firsthand experience of these horrors, is wise enough to apprehend them and to know the best remedy. He does not claim that work will *cure* all these evils. They are an abiding feature of the world in which we live. But work "keeps [them] away from us." An actively occupied person stands a better chance of keeping out of trouble—psychological, moral, financial, physical—than an idle one. The Turk's comment is no more profound than that.

This is perhaps a good juncture at which to ask ourselves whether there is evidence from outside *Candide* for taking the ending straight. And, of course, there is, if you once accept external biographical evidence, as Professor Wolper would readily agree (while arguing strongly that such evidence is quite invalid). Over and over Voltaire elsewhere advocates the value of work as an antidote to life's ills. One could cite a host of instances. For example, one of the closest parallels to Pococuranté occurs in another literary work, Voltaire's *Discours en vers sur l'homme* (1738), a collection of seven poetic epistles. In the fourth of these poems Voltaire evokes the spectacle of Brossoret, a rich man with nothing to do, bored to death, immune to the delights of love, poetry, music. Ennui is destroying him. Then suddenly, help arrives: "A god who took pity on human nature / Placed alongside Pleasure, Work and Pain: / Fear awoke him, Hope guided his steps . . ." (Moland, 9:405). Like Candide, Brossoret is saved by work from a death-in-life and begins to enjoy existence again. Now, there can be no question but that in this poem Voltaire is presenting the situation quite straightforwardly. The answer of the Wolper school to this and similar examples would be that we should not extrapolate from one situation to another. But the parallel is so close between Brossoret and Pococuranté that surely one must give it serious consideration. And if one is to be persuaded that in *Candide*, uniquely, Voltaire overturns one of the principles that guided him throughout his life, the textual evidence needs to be quite overwhelming. That evidence, however, stops a long way short of demonstrating the case for a totally revisionist reading of the tale.

One of the stronger planks in the Wolper argument is that the Turk's advice and Candide's decision to follow it represent a shallow anticlimax to all that has gone before. There is surely some merit in this. One could hardly argue that Voltaire has stumbled upon or is presenting a startling new truth. It is simply a matter of recognizing when one is well off. The king of Eldorado has already sounded that note very clearly when Candide and Cacambo decide to depart: "When you are fairly comfortable somewhere or other, you should stay there" (192). Then, it had fallen on deaf ears. Now, they are more receptive. It is not just the Turk's example of the good life that has persuaded Candide. Before that, the brusque philosophic advice of the dervish had also played its part. He points out to them the supreme indifference of whatever deity may exist toward human suffering: "When His Highness sends a ship to Egypt, is he concerned if the mice on the ship are comfortable or not?" (257). One should therefore stop philosophizing and simply "shut up." Agnosticism is the sole answer to the paradoxical and incomprehensible nature of good and evil.

The dismissively theoretical approach of the dervish ("reputed to be the best philosopher in Turkey" [256]), aided by the practical wisdom of the Turkish farmer, helps Candide to open his eyes. It is as if the same picture were presented twice, but with a totally different lighting. Candide is, as before, unable to afford more than this humble property because he has been cheated of so much; Cunégonde is still ugly and sour and will doubtless continue to be an intolerable wife; Pangloss will remain a failure in his own eyes, having failed to obtain a professorship in Germany. Doubtless, too, the boats will go on carrying the political unfortunates in Constantinople to exile or worse. But once the element of work for all is introduced into the equation, these miseries will be seen to have another side to them. Cacambo is no longer overworked; the land is productive; Cunégonde is good at pastry, and Giroflée at carpentry; Paquette can embroider; the Old Woman, though now infirm and presumably just as bad-tempered, looks after the linen. And so on. Where there was no structure, a meaning has been imposed.

But that meaning can hardly be termed definitive. Since the world of *Candide* is full of intractable evils, this cannot hope to be a wholly satisfactory answer. At any time thieves could break in to destroy and kill. An earthquake could just as easily occur in Constantinople as in Lisbon. But it is as suitable a spot as they are going to find, and geographically speaking, it has a special fitness, in being situated on the edge of Europe, for a hero who had to flee the Old World but found the New World (Eldorado always excepted) no better, and whose second exploration of Europe revealed, in a different perspective, just as much villainy as his first. The aim of the characters has been to survive. Here, they may just do so, if they are lucky. At least, while it lasts, they will live a tolerable existence. More than that no one has the right to ask or expect. There are no transcendental goals at which to aim. It is enough to have captured a little light in a dark world.

Flaubert, who admired *Candide,* considered this conclusion to be the work of a genius because, in his view, Voltaire captures the very sense of platitudinous existence: "this tranquil conclusion, *stupid as life is.*"[13] People who have run before the storm for so long can hardly hope for more. In advancing the work ethic, Voltaire was far from proposing a capitalist model, prefiguring the Industrial

Revolution. Work is not a universal panacea. It is not going to institute a new world of prosperity untinged by sorrows. This is just a tiny collection of people, trying to find a refuge from the horrors they have suffered. Voltaire adumbrates not an economic solution so much as a moral and psychological one, a modus vivendi to replace the European social order left behind as totally corrupt. At most, a few fragments from the wreck of the group's collective experience are being put together against total despair. But work is therapeutic and marginally more reliable than other means of survival; a modest step forward is being taken toward sanity and against both superstitious despair and optimistic nonsense. André Magnan argues well that nowhere in the tale is a new order of truth established, that there is no true conclusion, no moral message, just a tiny sign of encouragement to the community in the little garden.[14] The ending of *Candide* has no special value, and it is unwise to read the work on the assumption that it has.

Nor is the sociopolitical attitude emerging from *Candide* particularly radical either. Roland Barthes cogently sums it up as exemplifying the morality of the small individualist landowner, hostile to history and its rationalizations.[15] The period of Voltaire's political crusades was still to come, with only the episode of the black slave foreshadowing it here. Candide is no rebel. A reluctant fugitive, forever seeking peace and harmony in Cunégonde's arms, he at last puts together a viable answer somewhat better than what he has encountered on his travels (outside of Eldorado). It would be unwise to read too symbolic a meaning into his expulsion of the Baron from the garden. Candide has no intention of doing any such thing until the inflexible Baron forces it on him. In principle, the final community could well have accommodated an aristocrat, just as it accommodates a cleric, if the member of the nobility had been willing to accept changed circumstances. Voltaire's relations with the French aristocracy were far from hostile. Such nobles as the count d'Argental were among his closest friends. The distinction he drew was between those aristocrats who were socially useful and enlightened and those who were not. The Baron, unfortunately, belongs to the latter camp. The triumph in the last chapter, to the extent to which it can be called a triumph, is an individual one: Candide achieves personal autonomy. He finally frees himself of all father-figures: the Baron, Pangloss, Martin. By contrast, the Turk's advice at the end is merely a help to Candide in working out his own attitudes; the Turk thereafter immediately disappears from view. Voltaire, who believed himself to be an illegitimate child, had already richly exploited the father-son theme in earlier works.[16] *Candide* is finally a liberation from patriarchal authority of all kinds.

That said, one must add that Voltaire's political outlook evolves no further in terms of detail here. The organization of the little community near Constantinople is broadly participationist and egalitarian, each one contributing according to his talents. But Voltaire remains wholly vague on how it will settle down into permanent arrangements. How will they manage not to abuse Cacambo's propensity for hard work? Who will keep the accounts, and how will any profits be divided up? Can one count on Pangloss, for example, not to stand around all day leaning on his spade and reciting genealogies? And if one cannot, what is to be done about it? But to pose such questions is to demonstrate a totally aberrant view of *Candide*. There is no tidily wrapped-up ending, this is not a blueprint of a future civilization. It is just a makeshift arrangement, informed by a reasonable amount of common sense and hope. Candide himself enjoys a moral authority as the one who brought the group together by purchasing their freedom. He may just possibly develop into the seigneur in the fullness of time; the possibility is not excluded. But it is, equally, not considered either. That would be projecting onto *Candide* a perspective that *Candide* does not envisage.

Is there, then, a blueprint anywhere in *Candide*? What about Eldorado, which we have been excepting from the generalizations about other forms of society in the *conte*? It is certainly the case that Eldorado shows examples of what might be done. The place itself is beyond man's reach, but not all its achievements are equally unattainable. The development of science, the construction of handsome buildings, the exquisite courteousness of the inhabitants, were all within the capacity of enlightened eighteenth-century man. This is a society that supports the advancement of commerce; the hostelries set up to promote trade are state enterprises, funded by the government. Voltaire, who had admired the commercial spirit and energy of England in the *Lettres philosophiques*—a whole letter is devoted to singing the praises of trade—clearly considers this to be one of the most important aspects of Eldorado. Not only are the people well-mannered; their evident moral sanity springs from a rejection of dogmatic theorizing of all kinds. The landlord of the inn at which they put up responds to Candide's restless curiosity about how Eldorado fits in with the philosophy of optimism by remarking: "I am very ignorant, and all the better for it" (187). Voltaire had, ever since the *Lettres philosophiques*, praised the value of philosophic doubt and ignorance; a few years later, he was to compose a profession of his own attitudes under the title *Le Philosophe ignorant* (1766). In keeping with this spirit of tolerance in Eldorado, there are no divisive religious sects, no oppression of others, no churches, and no priests (at least in the European sense: the old man states that "we are all priests" since the king and all family heads sing hymns of thanksgiving every morning). The only religious practice consists of worshiping God and thanking Him for His blessings. All this represents an idealization of Voltaire's wishes for a deist society free of divisive doctrines and persecution. The Eldoradans are evidently people with whom one can maintain a wholly practical and realistic conversation. We are told that Candide and Cacambo talk to the old man at length about very down-to-earth topics like the form of government, customs, women, theater, and the arts. Besides, as has been pointed out earlier, Voltaire had contemporary Pennsylvania in mind as a model for much of what he has to say.

It needs to be noted, therefore, that more elements of Eldoradan society are set up as practical examples worthy of imitation than is sometimes allowed by commentators on *Candide*. The place, too, serves as a standing reproach to our greed-ridden and disputatious way of life. It thrives on dignified work, not on the mad pursuit of wealth for its own sake. Its people are simple and direct, unlike, for example, the hypocritical wretches of Paris.

But if the reader seeks to find the whole meaning of *Candide* in Eldorado he will be disappointed. The land is not only unreachable except by extraordinary accident. It is quite utterly different. Candide and Cacambo themselves register this point soon after their arrival when they wonder about "this country . . . where the whole of nature is of a kind so unlike ours" (186). The gold and jewels lying about everywhere on the ground, the longevity of life (the old man is 172 years old), the fast-running red sheep, the hoisting machine to take Candide and Cacambo over the mountains—all these belong to a fantasy world. Many of the details, seemingly gratuitous, add to the distancing effect. When the visitors ask about the religion of Eldorado, the old man replies that "we worship God from evening to morning" (188). What is one to understand by that? Do the Eldoradans never sleep, or do they perhaps take naps during the day? As the reader proceeds, his sense of bewilderment increases. The old man adds that when the king and all the heads of families sing hymns to God each morning, "five or six thousand musicians accompany them" (189). Here is another totally incomprehensible statement. Do all the patriarchs of Eldorado come together in the palace each morning? If so, at least some of them must have traveled nearly four hours to get there, for that is the time it takes our travelers to reach the capital. Or is the old man referring only to the inhabitants of the capital? Such speculation is futile. Mystery is intended to prevail on the matter. In simple guise, firm information is lacking on the sociopolitical structures of the country. We know that Eldorado is a monarchy, whose king is a man full of wit (a source of surprise to Candide, and the opportunity for a gibe by Voltaire at kings he had known). But the nature and extent of the powers he actually possesses are not made clear. He can evidently command instant obedience from 3,000 men for a crash program to build the hoisting machine. But how much freedom do his subjects actually enjoy? He tells the visitors that all men are free; yet in the distant past the leaders had decreed that no one should ever leave the kingdom. The right of movement, then, was given up at that time, by general consent in the first place. But what of the current generation? Do they ever have the chance at least to reconsider the pledge? We are told only that it would be a tyranny contrary to both their laws and their customs to detain foreigners. Beyond that, we are totally ignorant about the laws of Eldorado, other than that they are universally obeyed, for there are no law courts and no prisons.

Eldorado remains veiled in a kind of haze. We are not encouraged to look for total answers here. No program for ready adaptation to the countries of this world is available. It is more the *spirit* of Eldorado that others should observe and seek to imitate, a spirit based on the rejection of useless metaphysics, to the advantage of useful work for the common good. Voltaire had achieved something of the same kind many years before. In the *Lettres philosophiques* he had drawn a flattering picture of England, showing his French readers how much better things were across the Channel. That picture is sometimes distorted to the advantage of England, for polemical purposes. But Voltaire nowhere prescribes the importation of particular features of English life into France. Here too it is more a matter of showing how another culture can be superior to one's own. That approach has, of course, gone much further with Eldorado, which is, unlike contemporary England, a never-never land. But the strategies in each work are broadly comparable.

Unspecific though the king's prerogatives may be in Eldorado, he is the only authentic king on view in *Candide*. Not only, as we have seen, are there the mock-kings in Venice; royalty when it is effectively practiced can wear a menacing aspect. It is when Candide drinks to the king of the Bulgars that he leaves himself open to forcible impressment into that king's army. The king, it is true, saves him from being shot for desertion. But this is a sort of gratuitous act, dispensed by a personage so elevated that ordinary compassion hardly enters into it. Indeed, Voltaire hints that the "clemency" that the king displays is mainly for show, since it will be "praised in every journal down the ages" (124).[17] The true nature of that clemency is revealed very soon after, when the same king declares war on the king of the Abars, with the horrific consequences that Voltaire describes in the following chapter and that the king would have known to be the inevitable concomitant. But far from feeling any concern when the massacre actually happens, both kings proceed to the absurdity of singing a Te Deum to God after the battle, as though each were thanking God for being on his side. Political leaders live in a world of utter brutality and swift change of fortune, where their power and glory may just as easily collapse into farcical destitution (as the Venice carnival shows) or worse (as Candide and his companions observe from their little farm in Turkey). There are no honest princes in our world, only bullies or fools. Authority is mocked. No reliance may be placed on it, any more than upon the so-called philosophy of optimism. *Candide* offers no comforting answers, on either the political or the religious front.

6

Personal and Interpersonal

If politics and religion provide no consolation in *Candide,* what about the personal level? Can human beings find from each other the wherewithal to go on?

One false hope, repeatedly subverted, is provided by human sexual relations. It is desire that keeps Candide going, the promise of Cunégonde ever fresh until the final anticlimactic meeting in Turkey. Cunégonde is at the outset so attractive, and their first encounter so tantalizingly incomplete, that Candide's thoughts after being kicked out of Westphalia are only of her. When he meets the recruiting officers and they begin asking him, "Do you not love tenderly . . . ?" Candide interrupts eagerly, "Oh yes, I love tenderly Mademoiselle Cunégonde" (123). Wrapped up in his own passion, he is dangerously oblivious to the officers' real intentions. Later on, he is predictably appalled when falsely informed by Pangloss of Cunégonde's death; but he immediately wonders whether she died from a broken heart following his expulsion. The reality of her experiences is rather more crudely physical. Eventually, Candide knows a moment of pure delight when the Old Woman reunites him with his beloved in Lisbon. But here too he will encounter frustration. Their idyll on the sofa is brutally interrupted when Don Issachar rushes in. Fortunately for Candide, he has not divested himself of the sword that the Old Woman gave him, and thus he is able to dispatch his rival. But that is the end of any sweet exchanges, as the more urgent demands of self-preservation become of paramount importance. It is left unclear whether this love is subsequently consummated on the voyage to South America. Voltaire passes over the matter in silence as being of no consequence. In any event, Cunégonde seems less than overwhelmed by the romance when it comes to deciding whether to marry the governor of Buenos Aires. Nor is there even a moment of fond farewell when she and Candide have to separate. Thereafter and until the final pages, he will lead a life of yearning and his quest for his lost love.

But unlike in *Zadig*, where the hero finds his beloved Astarté again as lovely as ever, the world of *Candide* takes account of the effects of degeneration. When rediscovered, Cunégonde has deteriorated, both physically and temperamentally. Fine cakes will, it seems, be prepared by Cunégonde's skilled hands in the final Turkish garden; but of tender romantic union there appears to be no further hope whatsoever.

Thus also is it with the other sexual encounters. Paquette and Giroflée appear at first to be entranced with each other in Venice. The reality is otherwise. She is a prostitute who must feign love with her partners as part of her trade. He is a monk who detests the vocation imposed upon him by his parents and whose sole consolation is whoring. Sex is generally, throughout *Candide*, a venal or a brutal matter. Rape is a regular occurrence as soon as the social order breaks down: it happens to Cunégonde in the Westphalian château when it is invaded by the Bulgar troops, to the Old Woman on the corsairs' ship after being taken prisoner, and again on her arrival in Morocco. When anarchy gives way again to some semblance of civility, rape takes on a more civilized aspect, but it remains nevertheless forced submission of the female to the male will. Cunégonde lives a settled relationship with a Bulgar captain for three months until he tires of her; the Old Woman becomes the slave of a brutal Russian boyar, who beats her daily for two years until he is executed; Paquette is obliged to be the mistress of a doctor in return for his curing her of the pox, and then of a judge; and so on. Paquette's steady profession as a prostitute is but the regularization of these pitiless abuses of sexual power whenever women fall under the control of men. She eloquently describes the sordid misery of such a life: "exposed to every insult, every affront; reduced frequently to borrowing a skirt so as to have it pulled up by some disgusting man; robbed by one of what has been earned with another; held to ransom by officers of the law, and with nothing to look forward to except a horrible old age, a workhouse and one's body thrown on a dung heap" (228). The prostitution practiced in Paris is different in being more elegantly treacherous, but there too it is evidently a staple element of social life. Only in Eldorado, and then again at the Turkish farmer's home, is sexual immorality nonexistent. (Sexual behavior seems to have no explicit place in Eldorado: one more instance of its unreality.) It can hardly, therefore, be a matter of surprise when Pangloss points out that venereal disease is widespread, and that it is extending further afield all the time; the countries of the Orient would come to know it at first hand in the centuries ahead. As for the situation in Europe, adds Pangloss, "you can be sure that, when thirty thousand men fight a pitched battle against an equal number of troops, about twenty thousand on each side have the pox" (132).

Apart from Candide's pathetic passion, there are only two instances where sex does not lead to corruption or punishment. One occurs at Lisbon, where Cunégonde, by some extraordinary strength of personality, has managed to keep both Don Issachar and the Grand Inquisitor at bay and still acting as her protectors. She attributes this achievement of will to what she has suffered: "A person of honor may be raped once, but her virtue is strengthened by it" (145). However, the situation is fraught with uncertainty. Her two would-be lovers have time-shares in her company, but there have been rows over who owns her Saturday nights. The Inquisitor appears to be gaining the upper hand, and indeed the auto-da-fé has been put on by him, not just because of the earthquake but also to intimidate the Jew. It is altogether a highly volatile arrangement, unlikely to endure much longer than the six months it has already lasted when Candide resolves it by killing both men.

The other instance is the one place in *Candide* where Voltaire presents a scene of sexual tenderness; but it is over scarcely before it has begun. After Candide has shot the monkeys pursuing the two Oreillon girls, he discovers too late that this was a happy liaison and that the girls are distraught with grief. The incident serves of course as a satirical comment on Candide's naïveté, but it is also a sort of deconstruction of sexual fulfillment, which in *Candide* appears to work well only at a subhuman level, as between animal and human savage. Elsewhere it is an instrument of degradation or, at best, a false lure.

If sex is no remedy for the human condition, what about culture? In this panorama the cultivated life plays a relatively minor part. Indeed, in the harum-scarum section before Eldorado, when Candide is virtually always on the run, there is simply no place for patronage of the arts. Only in Eldorado does intellectual life seem to have acquired a meaningful function—though more in the sciences and town planning than in theater or the fine arts. By contrast, in the "real" world cultural activity seems sterile. The Bordeaux Academy of Sciences wallows in futility when trying to decide why the Eldoradan sheep is red. Paris is even worse. Candide weeps at scenes "perfectly played" in a new tragedy he is taken to, only to be told authoritatively that he is wrong to do so because the play and its actors are bad. (In the 1761 addition to this chapter, Voltaire develops at much greater length his attack upon fashionable criticism of the theater and also upon some of the new books appearing by authors hostile to him.) Venice offers the delights of carnival. But carnival serves only to highlight the sense that Venice is itself but a city of playacting and illusion, a triptych of false appearances in which the feigned happiness of Paquette and Giroflée links up with the charade of the six kings, across the central panel of Pococuranté's palace.

As we have already noted, the Pococuranté episode represents Voltaire's main depiction of the problem of boredom in *Candide*. To this we should add that Pococuranté's ennui is the more problematical for being set amidst untold wealth, which, furthermore, has been used to surround him with an exquisite environment—well-kept gardens, fine marble statues, a beautiful palace, old masters on the walls, an orchestra to play a delightful concerto as preparation for sitting down to an excellent dinner, and a superb library of the great authors. Yet he is bored to death by everything around him. He enjoys the favors of two pretty girls, but they too, as has happened with all the society women he has known, are beginning to pall on him. The arrival of Candide and Martin adds no luster to his day; he greets them with cool politeness. As for music and the arts, his judgment is almost unrelievedly condemnatory. The many paintings he owns leave him cold because they seem unnatural; even his two Raphaels are found unpleasing because of their dark colors and poor execution. Indeed, he confesses that he bought them some years before out of pure vanity. The music diverts him for a half-hour but no longer. He would prefer opera had it not become a monstrous collection of bad tragedies, ridiculous arias, and false acting. When it comes to literature, Homer's *Iliad* tediously depicts over and over the same unvarying battles and endlessly futile gods. It is true, some three books of Virgil's *Aeneid* are excellent, but most of it is tiresome. Pococuranté prefers Tasso and Ariosto, but as he gives no reason for the first and considers that Aristo too is boring, the preference seems to be gratuitous. Horace's poetry contains some useful maxims but is generally coarse and exaggerated. Cicero is set aside as totally useless. On the scientific front, the noble Venetian shares Voltaire's earlier dismissive view of the Academy of Sciences; the work of such academies is useless nonsense, without any pragmatic value to offer society. In the theater, the world has seen 3,000 plays, but not three dozen of them are any good. Books of sermons and theology are unreadable. Finally, Milton's *Paradise Lost* is singled out for denunciation as barbarous, obscure, bizarre, and disgusting.

It is worth setting out at length the full catalog of Pococuranté's criticisms because the portrait of this character is more complex than may at first appear. First of all, Voltaire himself had earlier voiced many of these comments. In particular, the opinions on Homer, Virgil, and Milton follow very closely Voltaire's own pronouncements in his *Essai sur la poésie épique* (1727). In addition, Pococuranté grudgingly agrees with Martin's favorable assessment of English books, even though he goes on to temper it with a depreciatory reference to the unduly zealous party spirit of English writers. More generally, Pococuranté intersperses his negative comments with remarks of which Voltaire could only approve. Having put down Horace, he concludes: "Fools admire everything in an esteemed writer. I read only for myself; I like only what is useful to me." Voltaire goes on to establish an immediate contrast with Candide, who is "very surprised at what he is hearing" because he "had been brought up never to judge of anything by himself" (234). The antithesis is clearly all to the benefit of Pococuranté, who will continue to establish his personal credentials with similarly enlightened statements. In agreeing on the value of English writings, he adds: "It is splendid to write what one thinks; that is man's privilege" (235). Later, he completes his vilification of Milton with the assertion that "I say what I think" (236), a favorite remark of Voltaire's in his correspondence.

With Pococuranté, therefore, we need to adopt a stance not dissimilar to that with Martin. Indeed, it is interesting to see that Martin "wholly agrees" with Pococuranté on opera and approves of his way of thinking as "quite reasonable" (234). The Venetian aristocrat is a formidable personality. Voltaire himself would write to his friend Thieriot two months after the publication of *Candide:* "I myself seem to have quite a bit in common with Signor Pococuranté" (D-8168). But, as with Martin, so too with Pococuranté one needs to retain a certain detachment. The closest parallels with his opinions from Voltaire's own writings appear in a work published over 30 years earlier. By contrast, Voltaire had extensively imitated Virgil in his own epic *La Henriade* (1723), expressed admiration for Cicero in the preface to his play *Rome sauvée* (1752), spoken warmly of Ariosto in the 1756 edition of his *Essai sur la poésie épique,* and had much praise for Horace in his letters around 1758.

What we have in Pococuranté is a self-questioning by the author. Virtually the same age as the 60-year-old Venetian (surely no coincidence), Voltaire too had faced the problems posed by a life of ease in comparative retreat from the world (on the edge of eighteenth-century Geneva, just as Pococuranté's palace can be reached by gondola from Venice). Voltaire's correspondence reveals the same preoccupations. Must a man of independent judgment, and free as Pococuranté is of crass materialism, end up with nothing to live for? Does indifference to worldly pleasures have to lead to disgust? One further aspect of the Venetian's thinking deserves to be emphasized. He believes that polite society is involved in a fraudulent conspiracy to conceal its fundamental boredom with culture. Having made the point that music may please for a half-hour but that thereafter it is tiresome, he adds, "although nobody dares to admit it" (232). The same accusation recurs at greater length when Homer is the topic: "I have sometimes asked scholars whether they were as bored as I am by reading him: all the honest ones admitted that the book fell out of their hands but that it was always necessary to have it in one's library as a monument of antiquity" (233). It is, one might argue, the cultural version of the mask of happiness that Voltaire also demystifies in *Candide.*

The capacity, then, of arts and letters to satisfy the human predicament is far from being wholly proven. Pococuranté's energies seem to be aroused only by gardening; tomorrow, he says, he will begin to reshape his estate to a more noble design. This is interestingly premonitory of the final garden outside Constantinople. Plantation seems a more promising alternative than the enjoyment of culture. No books or paintings are evident in the last chapter of *Candide*. Work must, in the immediate future at least, come first, so as to banish the prime enemy boredom. Culture and leisure will not of themselves achieve that. Voltaire's view of literature and the arts is much more complex and subtle than Pococuranté's. That does not preclude Pococuranté from bringing to the *conte* an element of fundamental skepticism about the values by which cultured society lives. The parallel with that other great contemporary work of self-doubt, Diderot's *Le Neveu de Rameau* (composed 1761–62; published 1823), seems well worth making.

But though the values of arts and letters may sometimes be falsified by the social world through oversimplification, more store may be set, in a modest way, by the virtues of taking meals together. The importance of food in *Candide* has been noted by Christopher Thacker, who, in his edition of the story, comments, "At every stage there is eating and drinking."[1] Food, or the lack of it, illustrates the progress of Candide's career. Chased out of the "earthly paradise" in Westphalia, he is soon "dying of hunger" (122). That is why he stops by the inn where the recruiting officers exploit his starvation in order to impress him into the Bulgar army. The battle between the Bulgars and Abars, precipitating Candide's flight from the scene, reduces him to hunger once more by the time he reaches Holland. His refusal to agree that the Pope is the Antichrist condemns him to go on starving, so far as the Protestant minister and his wife are concerned. Only the good Anabaptist Jacques has the charity to recognize him as a fellow human being and to give him food and beer. Two months of comfortable living follow, to end in the Lisbon disaster. Candide, knocked down by stones hurled through the air in the earthquake, calls on Pangloss to find him "a little wine and oil" (136). The latter, preoccupied with trying to explain the earthquake in terms of optimism, ignores the request until Candide loses consciousness, at which point Pangloss at last rouses himself to bring his companion a little water, a poor substitute worthy of that impractical philosopher. But the next day they find some food to keep them going in the debris, and thereby fortified a little, they work at helping the survivors of the earthquake, for which they are rewarded by a modest dinner from their grateful companions.

However, the meal serves as the occasion of another downfall. Pangloss returns the wrong religious answers to his neighbor the Inquisitor, and both he and Candide are arrested at the end of the meal, to be carried off to the auto-da-fé. Candide, abandoned since Pangloss is apparently dead from his hanging, is fortunate enough to encounter the Old Woman, who restores his strength by regular meals over the following days prior to reuniting him with Cunégonde. Thereafter, when he has heard her story, they enjoy a meal together and subsequent dalliance on the sofa. But the moment is short-lived; once more Candide must flee, at first with Cunégonde and the Old Woman to Buenos Aires, thereafter to Paraguay with Cacambo.

At last, in Paraguay, there is a moment of peace and joy. Once more, starvation (Cacambo tells the Jesuits that the two of them are dying of hunger) is assuaged, and this time splendidly out of golden bowls and rock crystal goblets, as befits the general air of arrogance about the place; the Paraguayans meanwhile eat plain corn out in the open fields. Things improve still further for the visitors when they recognize the Reverend Father Commandant to be the young Baron, Cunégonde's brother. "As they were German," comments Voltaire ironically, "they stayed at table for a long time" (172). But it is another false dawn. After the Baron is left for dead from Candide's sword thrust, Cacambo engineers the swiftest of escapes. He has been alert enough to think about food for the journey, so they are well provided with bread, chocolate, ham, fruit, and wine; Cacambo thinks it makes simple common sense, once they have succeeded in making good their flight, to stop for a meal. We have noticed earlier the comic aspects of this particular meal and how it reinforces the general tone of *Candide*. Hunger is eventually appeased—in Candide's case, despite himself. But then the Oreillons episode overtakes them and they are in danger for a while of being eaten themselves, though reconciliation is eventually achieved over the "refreshments" that the Oreillons give them. That, however, is but the prelude to their adventure in the wilderness, where once again they run out of food and have to live off wild fruits and water for a whole month, before Eldorado comes to their rescue.

As one might expect, Eldorado entertains the travelers lavishly to delicious food, exquisitely served. But unlike the Paraguayan settlement, there is no hint of inequality, and the hospitality is backed up by "extreme courtesy." This quality of service is no accident; the hostelry offering it is part of a state-run service. The reception of guests occupies a high place of priority in the civic and commercial values of Eldorado, as is confirmed by the excellent welcome extended by the king to the newcomers to dine at his own table. But when "the happy pair decided to be happy no longer" by leaving Eldorado, they have to face all over again the hazards of life in the outside world. At least starvation is a thing of the past, thanks to the wealth they have brought out of Eldorado. Candide's experiences at table become more subtle, not simply a means of survival. But the perils, though of a different order now, still remain. Parisian suppers are accompanied, as we have seen, by cheating or calumny; only the exceptional man of learning and taste speaks his mind honestly at these tables. In Venice meals are reserved for learning the truth behind the mask, first when Paquette tells her wretched personal story, later when the six kings recount their equally miserable experiences in public life. In between, Pococuranté hosts an excellent dinner, but it is equally hollow in significance because he is tired of everything.

After all these variations on the theme of food, the way is clear for the only genuine hospitality that Candide receives, apart from the welcomes by Jacques and in Eldorado, both of them in their different ways too good for this world. The Turkish farmer offers exotic, delicate fruit, sorbets, and coffee, reinforcing by his generous gesture the essential sanity of his advice. The incentive to work in the garden takes on specific qualities. Candide and his friends may also, with the help of fortune, enjoy before long the exotic delights of eating pistachios and citrons cultivated by their own hands.

Food therefore acts as a leitmotiv, an index of destitution (when it is lacking) as well as of social exchanges of various kinds. For all the fantastic aspects of the plot, the realistic attention paid to details of food is an important feature throughout. The commensality of dining together can be a beacon of hope in a generally dark world. Like friendship, to which it is frequently related, it offers consolation, often modest and sporadic, but one more reason for not taking Martin's unrelieved pessimism at face value.

These meals, besides, are not shared by mere puppets. The characters in *Candide* are generally caricatural, it is true. But one would be unwise to assume as a logical consequence that they are merely simplistic two-dimensional figures, mechanically predictable in all they say and do. Like the world they inhabit, these characters are much given to surprising paradoxes. We have already noted the complex ambivalences in Pococuranté's makeup: he represents a nightmare possibility to be conjured by the author. Similarly, the function of Jacques in the *conte*, despite his brief appearance, repays closer study.

Jacques is an Anabaptist, a member of a sect for which Voltaire had considerable respect. In the historical work *Essai sur les moeurs*, Voltaire describes Anabaptists as "the most peaceful of all men, taken up with their manufactures and trading, hard-working, charitable" (Moland, 12:302). In these respects, Jacques is basically like the good Quaker whom Voltaire had met in England and later described in the first of his *Lettres philosophiques:* modest, direct, honest, pacific, tolerant, and a successful merchant. As with the Manichean creed and Martin, the technical details of Anabaptism need not detain us. (To cite one paradox: as a Christian, albeit of an unorthodox kind, Jacques ought to believe in Original Sin, which does not, however, seem to enter into his philosophy of human nature.) The theological merit of Anabaptists in Voltaire's eyes, as he indicates in his *Essai sur les moeurs*, was that they were of Unitarian tendency, recognizing only God as divinity (while yet revering Christ) and managing to exist on the minimum of dogma and dispute. Like the Quakers, therefore, they represented a viable way of life that, while not entirely compatible with Voltaire's own deist beliefs, held out some hopes of a better existence in society. What matters essentially about Jacques is that he incarnates practical goodness. When he meets Candide for the first time, the latter has just been befouled with the unnamed stuff poured upon him by the orator's good wife. But Jacques is neither amused nor disgusted. He recognizes beneath this abomination "one of his brothers, a being with two feet and no feathers, and possessing a soul" (128). This wholly ecumenical approach inspires immediate benevolence, in a sensible order of practical priorities; Candide is taken home, cleaned up, given bread and beer, bestowed with a little money, and then set to useful employment in Jacques's textile mill. The same spontaneous generosity will operate when Pangloss appears: "The good man did not hesitate to give hospitality to Doctor Pangloss" (132). Not only that; Jacques cures Pangloss at his own expense. Here Voltaire is doubtless recollecting his own act of charity when he also cured someone of venereal disease, and also at his own expense.[2]

But these acts of goodwill are not purely altruistic in motive. Jacques's belief in charity has a pragmatic aspect. He is a hard-headed factory owner, able to use skilled labor such as Candide and Pangloss represent. Pangloss's fine handwriting and his arithmetical skills, never mentioned or exploited elsewhere in *Candide*, make him an ideal bookkeeper. By helping Pangloss and Candide, Jacques is also helping himself. It is such a policy of enlightened self-interest that is most likely to lead to prosperity and happiness. Jacques possesses, as any merchant might, a strong dislike of bankruptcy, which he lists as one of the worst of human misdeeds, second only to warmongering. In this he echoes Voltaire's view, set down in the *Lettres philosophiques*, of the London Stock Exchange, where the only infidels, regardless of religious creed, are those who go bankrupt. Jacques, one feels, would have made an excellent member of that English institution. His commonsensical sort of generosity is seen in his actions on meeting Candide; Jacques gives him money, but just two florins to tide him over. It is this clear-eyed view of the proper function of money in society that helps to make him such a good businessman. Besides, in keeping with the modern merchant, as Voltaire describes him in the *Lettres philosophiques*, Jacques is a cosmopolitan, interested in pursuing trade beyond his own national borders. Hence the motive for his visit to Lisbon. Commerce has a place of honor in a healthy society, as Eldorado will bear out when Candide's courteous fellow guests at the hostelry turn out to be mainly from the world of business. Whatever the success of the final garden in Turkey turns out to be, it is at least framed on sound principles in growing produce for sale in Constantinople.

To the end, Jacques is an activist. When the storm is unleashed in Lisbon harbor, anarchy breaks out: "Those who could worked, nobody listened to anyone, no one was in control." But Jacques, as a man of natural enterprise, aims to be useful; he "was trying to be of some help in steering the ship" (134). That is why he is on the deck, and it is presumably because he is in this prominent position that he attracts the violent wrath of the rascally sailor. So too his active efforts lead to his death, when he tries to save the sailor who has fallen overboard. Voltaire will immediately add an ironic counterpoint when Pangloss prevents Candide from going to Jacques's rescue, the philosopher invoking optimist fatalism in support of his own passivity.

Jacques, as we know, is the only important character in *Candide* who definitively dies. (He is not, however, unique: the old Baron, his wife, and the wicked Vanderdendur also perish; but none of them lays the same claim on our attention.) Death is for others to suffer. The principal business of the major characters in the *conte* is to survive. Why, then, does Voltaire single out Jacques in this exceptional way? There is no clear-cut answer, but some hypotheses suggest themselves. It may be because Voltaire cannot share Jacques's Rousseauist view of human nature. But, as we noted earlier, the author's own attitudes in this respect are not totally consistent, and that would surely be making too much of one short speech. Once again, we should beware of turning *Candide* into a philosophical treatise. It is Jacques as practical helper, not as thinker, who essentially counts, and as such he wins Voltaire's unqualified approval. If Jacques is removed from the scene so early and so totally, the reason is more likely to be that any such character is too positive in a work where positive examples have little place. One does not have to reflect for long to realize that a *conte* in which Jacques remains physically upon the scene could not have maintained the outlook and style of *Candide*. The heroes of *Micromégas* and *Zadig* are totally praiseworthy; that is part of the reason for the relatively lesser achievements of these two stories. The only true hero possible in *Candide* is an originally foolish boy who gradually learns some basic truths about the world.

That said, the values represented by Jacques will live on even though Jacques may not. Unlike the parodic, ultimately meaningless resurrections of Pangloss and the Baron, something of

Jacques's attitudes will survive, implicitly, in the final garden. His model of a merchant-based community, echoed in Eldorado, will be followed, however falteringly, by the tiny group at the end.

As for the three important female characters, they serve to remind us throughout that, even though virtuous characters of either sex are not likely to prosper in *Candide,* the rules of this world have been devised by men, who generally abuse and oppress women as they wish. Two of the three (Paquette and the Old Woman) function mainly as narrative voices recounting their past miseries. In Paquette's case the tone is somber and dignified, even unrealistically so if we reflect that she hardly speaks in the style of a lower-class prostitute.[3] Her life has been a struggle for existence. Otherwise, we know very little about her. Evidently, she is no tragic heroine, whatever her misfortunes. Like Giroflée, she fails to come and thank Candide for his generous gift of money to her—a point that merely confirms Martin's skepticism about the wisdom of the gift in the first place. (The gesture, munificent but foolish, under-lines by implicit contrast the good sense of Jacques's earlier help to Candide, frugal but geared realistically to a precise situation and an expectation of work.) Martin had predicted that the money was likely to add to their unhappiness, and he is proved right. The life of Paquette and Giraflée since then, as becomes clear when they reappear in the final scene, has been one of separations and recon-ciliations, quarrels, prison, flight. Paquette's former dignity seems to have deserted her, and she is no longer even successful as a prostitute. Her life has touched its nadir, just as the very arrival of the couple signals the lowest point for the rest of the little commu-nity. Fortunately, she can embroider; so for her too there is a useful place at the end.

The Old Woman plays her main part in the two chapters where she recounts her life story, and it is there that she is given the supreme compliment of enunciating a viewpoint on human exis-tence that coheres with the tone of the *conte.* Otherwise, her role is sketchy. But as with Paquette, though to a greater degree, she is allowed no possibility of pathos. The very grotesqueness of her being minus one buttock sets her apart.

This loss neither impedes her actions nor causes her any apparent distress or pain. She is able, for instance, to ride on horseback to Cadiz (including 30 miles at one go) just as well as

Candide and Cunégonde, "although I can sit upon only one buttock" (150). In her own narrative she brushes over the most horrific incidents as though they were of no concern to her. As servant to Cunégonde, she is totally unsentimental. Basically she is disposed to be helpful when she can, and she does much to revive Candide after the auto-da-fé. But she has no hesitation in jettisoning him when he becomes too great a burden in Buenos Aires. She is in some respects a female counterpart of Cacambo, lacking his cheerfulness but, like him, not disposed to philosophize when the situation requires action. While Candide and Cunégonde are wringing their hands in despair because of the double murder he has committed, it is the Old Woman who points out that there are three fine horses in the stable and that Cunégonde has money and jewelry. She is totally insensitive to the young couple's fearful bewilderment: "The weather couldn't be finer, and it's a great pleasure to travel during the cool of the night" (149). It is she who later on spots the thief who has made off with their possessions, and who again calms the others' apprehensions by taking the initiative. They will sell one of the horses, and "I shall ride behind Mademoiselle, although I can sit upon only one buttock" (150). Her anatomical singularity becomes ever stranger. She is clearly indomitable, but so as to remove her into a comic universe that our sympathies are precluded from reaching. When she reappears with Cunégonde at the end, she too has deteriorated; she has become bad-tempered and above all conscious that boredom is the worst of all evils. But in the new dispensation she will look after the laundry, a clear-cut role that should with luck keep the demon of ennui at bay.

Cunégonde's function in *Candide* is, of course, much more important. She is, after all, the "heroine" of the *conte*. For most of the story she fits that situation admirably, from her first appearance in the Edenic château—just 17, virginal and utterly desirable, with an adolescent's curiosity about Pangloss's lovemaking and a readiness to initiate Candide into similar delights. But her desire to become Candide's "sufficient reason" is cruelly thwarted, and the Cunégonde we next meet has endured the horrors of rape and servitude, not to mention seeing her parents massacred. Cunégonde, however, matches the Old Woman in resilience. As she puts it paradoxically, "A person of honor may be raped once, but her virtue is strengthened by it" (145). She has learned how to hold at bay powerful men like Don Issachar and the Grand Inquisitor. Nor is she distraught at memories of the past; indeed, there were some consolations. The Bulgar captain who became her protector found her very pretty, "I have to confess" (144), she interpolates rather complacently; for her part she sensuously recalls that he was very handsome, with a soft white skin. No sign of any grieving for the lost Candide, or indeed for her lost innocence! To be sure, when she rediscovers Candide naked and being flogged in the auto-da-fé she avows that "it was the height of horror, consternation, pain, despair." But these words ring a little strangely when she goes on immediately to add: "I shall tell you, truly, your skin is even whiter and more perfect in color than that of my Bulgar captain" (146). The fact that that skin was in the process of being beaten into a bloody pulp seems to weigh less with her than the rediscovery of his sexual attractiveness.

A girl with a healthy appetite, one might say, and not too burdened by the more delicate sensibilities. Her lack of imaginative sympathy is quickly evident. Although she sheds a tear or two when Candide tells her about Jacques's death, she still feels that no one has ever suffered as she has done. After all, not only has she known horrors and outrages; as she reminds the Old Woman, she who was born a baroness with 72 quarterings has been reduced to the status of a mere cook. It is this haughty assurance of the unparalleled nature of her miseries that incites the Old Woman to tell her own story. Cunégonde has still to learn from the latter, confirmed by all the other transatlantic passengers, that unhappiness is universal. But this discovery changes nothing in her attitudes to the world. When the governor of Buenos Aires asks for her hand in marriage, her love for Candide does not appear to be an insuperable barrier. On the contrary, she needs only a quarter of an hour, she tells the governor, to make up her mind and to consult the Old Woman. Doubtless she is aware that it will not take any longer for the latter to size up the situation and deliver her judgment. And doubtless too she, like the title character of Antoine François Prévost's *Manon Lescaut* (1731), would have happily settled for keeping her true lover as paramour while fulfilling her sexual obligations elsewhere.

But the arrival of the Spanish police quickly rules out that possibility, and once more Candide has to flee precipitately. He is distraught at leaving Cunégonde. What, he wonders, will become of her? But if Cunégonde sheds any tears at parting from Candide we do not hear of it; furthermore, the sagacious Cacambo is clearly skeptical on that point. She'll be all right, he replies to Candide's solicitous concerns about her: "Women are never at a loss; God provides" (168). Thus the hardheaded Cunégonde disappears from the story until near the end. She will remain only in a quite different guise, as the fantasy-object of Candide's sentimental dreams, the absent one amid all the delights of Eldorado, the reason for his remorse when he is unfaithful to her in Paris. He is transported with delight at the prospect of meeting her in the French capital and, when he has recovered from the disappointment of discovering that he has been tricked, at the expected reunion in Venice. But the pleasure of reconciliation is to be deferred until Constantinople.

Then, before he is reunited with her Candide is informed by Cacambo that Cunégonde's beauty has vanished. Even so, it remains his duty, he says, to love her forever. Only the sight of her will bring home the reality of her terrible ugliness: "[Candide] stepped back three paces, seized with horror, then approached her out of politeness" (252). Worse still, no one has told her she is ugly. So she demands that Candide keep his promises, with a peremptoriness that is merely a development of her earlier egoism, but now without any remaining charms of youthfulness. This physical degeneration parallels the decline in her moral influence over Candide. Where she had been the sought-after ideal, she has now become a disagreeable necessity. When it comes to deciding what to do with the Baron, she is not even informed until he has been expelled. At this point she is the most marginal of the little group; not surprisingly, as she grows uglier with every passing day she becomes quite intolerable. She plays no part in the subsequent discussions and visits. Only once is she mentioned again, when we learn in the final paragraph that she has turned into an excellent pastry cook. So she will, like the others, have a useful role in the garden. But no one represents better than Cunégonde, by her very function in the *conte*, the transmutation of the fallacious ideal into anticlimactic but practical reality.

By contrast, the part played by Cacambo demonstrates robust common sense, with a strong admixture of kindness, from start to finish. He is not, like Jacques, too good for the world of *Candide*. He always has his feet firmly on the ground. Yet his quick-witted pragmatism is not, as it is in the case of the Old Woman, made subservient to narrow self-interest. As we have seen, he is the living disproof of Martin's cynical pessimism. He represents the natural energy of the free man, who knows his own worth and his own values. Indeed, he strikingly anticipates the great dramatic creation by Pierre Beaumarchais, himself a devoted admirer of Voltaire, some 20 years later: Figaro. Like Figaro, he has been everywhere, done everything: "He had been a choirboy, sacristan, sailor, monk, agent, soldier, lackey." His attitudes are straightforward and morally sound: he "liked his master very much, because his master was a very good man." But he does not waste his time crying over spilled milk. If they are obliged to leave Buenos Aires, well then, the sooner the better: "Let us flee without looking behind us" (168); the advice has a symbolic as well as a purely literal truth about it. He knows Paraguay already, having once been a kitchen valet there, and he sums up the Jesuit colony with a broadside that destroys its pretensions before we even see it: "Los Padres have everything there, and the people nothing; it is the very masterpiece of reason and justice" (169). Voltaire lends Cacambo the full ferocity of his wit as the latter goes on to develop a piquant contrast between Jesuits killing the Spanish in Paraguay and sending them to heaven in Madrid by hearing their confessions.[4] Cacambo indulges a broad sense of humor at this marvelous example of human, religious, and political absurdity.

Cacambo is useful, too, in Paraguay because he speaks Spanish (being himself a mixture of Spanish and Indian breeding), so he naturally takes the initiative. It is thanks to Cacambo that they get the food they desperately need, when the Jesuits learn that Candide is not Spanish but German; it is Cacambo who makes sure their horses are kept close to them "just in case" (171). Which is most fortunate when the quarrel breaks out and Candide deals the Baron an apparently lethal thrust with his sword. Once again, as in Buenos Aires, a quick getaway is essential; not only that, Candide will need to be disguised as a Jesuit. Cacambo is just the man for such brilliant presence of mind. He is also versed in the ways of the world, explaining to Candide that it is quite common for monkeys to be lovers of girls. But unlike Martin, he does not exult over Candide's ignorance. Instead, in typically practical fashion, he foresees that by killing the monkeys Candide may well have landed them in trouble. So it turns out. However, Cacambo does not share Candide's temptation to easy despair; nor does he set any store by telling the Oreillon savages, as Candide advises him, that it would be un-Christian to cook them in the pot. He has a Voltairean taste for the paradox. Readily conceding the point that it is perfectly fair to eat one's enemies, he points out to the Oreillons that in fact they are mistaken, for they are about to dine off their friends. To persuade them of what he is saying, he urges them to confirm it empirically with the Jesuits. Here in Cacambo, as with the heroes of the earlier Voltaire stories *Zadig* and *Micromégas*, positive verification is proved superior to the affirmation of empty generalities.

This paragon of rational sanity, once the two are released from the Oreillons' hands, now urges Candide to return to Europe, since it is clear, he says, that the Western Hemisphere is no better than the eastern one. But it is because Candide wishes to remain on the continent where Cunégonde lives that this advice is not taken up and that, heading for Cayenne, they lose their way and end up in Eldorado. Nor would they even have reached that destination if Cacambo had not suggested that their only remaining resource in their desperate state was to drift down the river, since a river always leads to habitation eventually.

However, once in Eldorado, Cacambo is as bewildered as Candide—another index of the exceptionality of that country. He is deceived into thinking that the children playing with gold and precious stones must belong to the king. He commits the solecism of trying to pay for his meal in the inn. He imagines all kinds of ridiculous postures they might have to undertake when greeting the king. Like Candide, he wants to exchange this blissful existence for the real world again. Only in knowing Peruvian, the language of Eldorado, is Cacambo able to show any of his customary initiative. Eldorado, quite simply, is not a land where his admirable qualities can have any effective purchase on reality.

With their emergence from Eldorado, Cacambo's role as a major figure comes to an end. He leaves Surinam for Venice, where he hopes to reunite Candide with Cunégonde through buying off the governor of Buenos Aires with the immense wealth he is carrying on him. Cacambo, Voltaire informs us, is in despair at parting from his master and friend; but he is consoled at the thought of being capable of doing him a service. One might be pardoned for the cynical thought that, with all that money, consolation would be fairly easy to achieve. But as we have noted, that would be falling into the same facile fatalism practiced by Martin. Voltaire is here subverting our expectations in the opposite direction. In *Candide*, as in the world it portrays, good deeds can occur against all expectations.

When Cacambo reappears, it is in a more somber context. He is now a slave, and he has obviously suffered from his privations, as witness his face "the color of soot" (238). All his money has been stolen from him. Furthermore, he has, like Cunégonde and the Old Woman, been led from pillar to post by the pirate who captured them. Candide purchases his freedom and Cacambo joins the little band; but now his situation is much less prominent. Indeed, at first he is left to cultivate the garden on his own, crushed and in despair (as never before in the *conte*) at his fate. Eventually, one must assume, he is content with his lot when the working arrangements are revised. But curiously, he is the only character not mentioned in the final dispositions. Cacambo's main function has been played out earlier, with a friendless Candide, still poor and on the run. After Eldorado Candide's explorations take a different turn and require more complicated situations.

By contrast, Pangloss is present in the flesh or in spirit from beginning to end. He makes his first appearance in the fourth paragraph of the opening chapter, and it is he who utters the penultimate observations in the *conte*, to which Candide laconically replies in the famous closing remark. All commentators on Pangloss point out, as indeed they must, his clownish stupidity as the exponent of optimism. He stamps his identity indelibly upon the reader with his first "demonstration," that noses were made to hang spectacles on. But there is more to Pangloss than this. He is also, as we have seen, a menace when his recourse to quietist passivity results in Jacques's death. However, that is not all. It is piquant that this apostle of an apparently cheerful philosophy should suffer from venereal disease. For venereal disease is not only horrible in its effects, as the spectacle of Pangloss reappearing in Holland amply illustrates. It is one of the most eloquent critiques of divine harmony that the act of reproducing the human race should incur this awful consequence. When Candide inquires as to the reason for his dreadful state, Pangloss replies: "Alas . . . it is love, the comforter of the human race, the custodian of the universe, the soul of all sensitive beings, tender love" (130). He then proceeds to establish a genealogy of the disease, reaching back to Columbus's companions. But when Candide tentatively suggests that the Devil must be responsible for such a horror, Pangloss has of necessity to demonstrate the very opposite. This, he argues, is a necessary ingredient in the best of all possible worlds. For though he himself points out that venereal disease not only poisons the source of reproduction but often prevents reproduction altogether, he balances it against the gains that Columbus's discovery of the New World brought us: chocolate and cochineal. Yet it is he who also states that two-thirds of all the mercenaries in all the armies are infected. Nothing can show more clearly the blinkered state of Pangloss's thinking. He is not ignorant of the medical or social facts. But it changes nothing; "whatever is, is right," as Pope had said. Thereafter, you devote your intellectual energies to searching for any advantages, however derisory, like spectacle-fitting noses or chocolate.

This inclination to philosophical debate is a dangerous faculty for Pangloss to possess once he has left the safe haven of Westphalia, and his attempt to reconcile liberty with absolute necessity leads directly to the Inquisition and the auto-da-fé. Thereafter he disappears from the scene except as an ideal mentor to whom Candide continually appeals, absent but present (as is Cunégonde on the sentimental plane). Only with the closing scenes does he return, still in Candide's view "the most profound metaphysician in Germany," but sadly reduced to the role of a galley slave. It turns out that Pangloss, for all his near-escape from death by hanging and the traumas of surgical dissection, still possesses the vitality to be attracted by the pretty young girl he encounters at her prayers in a Constantinople mosque. Not only is she praying in this most unlikely situation (seeing that women are, by the rules of Islam, forbidden to enter a mosque); to add to the absurd unreality, "her bosom was entirely uncovered"; between her two breasts reposed "a beautiful bouquet of tulips, roses, anemones, buttercups, hyacinths, and auricula" (250). It is probably the most erotic scene in a *conte* that, for all its reputation in this respect, is generally far removed from sexual titillation. Described in some detail by

Pangloss, it serves to stress once again his lustful temperament. Just as his philosophical optimism ensured that he would be forever unteachable on that score, so it is that in love also he cannot help himself. In this holy place and in the very presence of the old imam who is the officiating priest, Pangloss replaces the bouquet that the girl has (somewhat suspiciously) let fall. But he takes his time, eagerly, over this delightful act of gallantry, and naturally it lands him in trouble once again. He utterly fails to see why. When he joins up with the Baron on the galley, Pangloss stoutly maintains that it is much more permissible to replace a bouquet upon a woman's breast than to be discovered naked, as the Baron had been, with a young man. For Pangloss with his rigid principles, the normative, of course, always applies; heterosexuality must necessarily be better than homosexuality, regardless of the fact that Pangloss's action had been provocative to an extreme. But to argue that Pangloss is only a desiccated philosopher is to miss much of the comic element in his makeup at moments like this. His philosophic apology for the status quo and propensity for fatalism seem to take second place to urgent sexual desire when an attractive woman is at hand.

So things move toward their conclusion. When asked for his opinion about whether Candide should marry Cunégonde, Pangloss predictably uses abstract principles of justice and the totally irrelevant laws of the Holy Roman Empire to arrive at the futile conclusion that the marriage should be morganatic—as if questions of property inheritance had any meaning in their marginal situation. It is no surprise, then, that someone who has been knocked about all over Europe should nevertheless have retained the norms of his earlier years. If he is in despair, it is not for immediate reasons like boredom or overwork. Instead, he bears the frustrated hopes of one who had wished to be a brilliant philosopher in a German university. Such is his limited view of the world. The lack of realism informing his philosophy spreads to everything about him. Yet, when meeting Paquette again, even he cannot resist a sigh at what he has suffered through being infected by her: "Ah! what is this world?" At last, he confesses that he "had always suffered horribly." That said, this new awareness of the past realities of his life cannot change anything; "but having once maintained that everything functioned marvelously, he maintained it forever, and did not believe a word of it" (256).

Pangloss is a hollow character, within an impervious outer carapace. He is doomed to plough the same furrow over and over until he dies. There can be no doubt that optimism goes down to total defeat along with its champion. And yet. . . . The last two paragraphs of the *conte* leave a more complex final impression of Pangloss than is often allowed by the critics. When Candide, after the visit to the Old Turk, expresses his belief that the latter is much better off than the six kings with whom he had dined in Venice, Pangloss in reply puts on a veritable display of pyrotechnics. High office is very dangerous, he claims, and he proceeds to illustrate his remark with reference to no fewer than 32 kings, princes, emperors, and other leaders of times past—starting with the Old Testament and ending with the German emperor Henry IV—who were assassinated or otherwise suffered harsh fates. What is more, on strict fact Pangloss is generally correct, as the Pomeau edition (259, n. 9) makes clear. Voltaire confers upon his character the immense learning that he had himself acquired in his historical researches for his *Essai sur les moeurs*. To all this cascade of erudition Candide replies very simply, while neatly transferring the discussion from the unchangeable past to the immediate present: "I also know . . . that we must cultivate our garden" (259). But Pangloss is not to be so easily silenced: " 'You are right,' said Pangloss; 'for when man was put into the garden of Eden, he was put there, *ut operaretur eum*,[5] for him to work; which proves that man was not born to seek repose' " (259–60).

So they all set to work, with happy results as so many individual talents are uncovered. But once again it is Pangloss who has to offer a commentary. "Pangloss would sometimes say to Candide: 'All events are linked together in the best of all possible worlds; for after all, if you had not been expelled from a beautiful castle and your backside well and truly kicked because of your love for Mademoiselle Cunégonde, if you hadn't been put to the Inquisition, if you hadn't run around America, if you hadn't delivered a great sword thrust to the Baron, if you hadn't lost all your sheep from the fine country of Eldorado, you would not now be eating preserved citrons and pistachios.' " It is the same lunatic equation we noted earlier: cochineal in exchange for venereal disease, citrons for

Candide's series of misfortunes. Note too the repetitive quality of this homily: "Pangloss *disait* quelquefois." Nothing is definitively settled. All Candide can do is to be polite while reiterating what he has said before: " 'That is well said,' replied Candide, 'but we must cultivate our garden' " (260).

What are we to make of these late interventions by Pangloss? To assume that he is just a buffoon does not do full justice to the situation. He is, first of all, a great storehouse of historical data. At various points in the *conte,* as we have seen, he demonstrates his knowledge of the history of venereal disease, of Roman law, and of assassinated princes. Where he goes wrong is at the point when he tries to relate all this information to the general theory of optimism. Then the blinkers descend.[6] Even so, Pangloss is indefatigable. His brand of folly will not go away, all the more so because it is based on such a formidable array of learning. Candide and the others will have to go on living with his aberrations—one more reason for not seeing the *conte* as ending upon some golden dawn. Pangloss represents the constant menace of the ivory tower intellectual who, for all his scholarship, works complacently within a preordained system of values. It is much more comfortable that way. But such an approach visits despair upon the world, and abstract dogmas always carry the threat of intolerance and oppression, even if Pangloss himself does nothing worse than allow Jacques to die. Whereas Candide's tentative but practical initiatives in an uncertain world represent the only true way forward.

What, then, of the hero himself? Whereas the other characters come and go, Candide is present from the first sentence to the last. Even when someone else is narrating his or her adventures, he is in the audience. His evolution provides the unity of the *conte.* From the start, he has no fixed place in the universe, for he is a bastard and motherless, kept in the château on sufferance. The moment he undertakes an act of personal initiative in kissing Cunégonde's hand, he learns quite brutally that he has no rights in this place. The earthly paradise is for others (at least temporarily) but not for him. Very quickly he will discover that in the cold outside world his lack of freedom is even more cruelly confirmed. Having decided to leave the Bulgar army, "thinking that it was a privilege of the human species, as of the animal species, to make use of his legs however he liked" (123), he finds that this privilege is no longer available to him. His only freedom in practice is a derisory one: would he prefer to run the gauntlet of the whole regiment 36 times or receive a dozen bullets in his brain? The instinct for survival dictates the former option, but after two "promenades" and 4,000 blows from the regiment, even death is preferable, and only the fortuitous appearance of the Bulgar king saves him.

Desertion, however, becomes possible after the battle between the Bulgars and the Abars, though it carries the same penalties as when Candide fled from Westphalia: hunger and destitution. This is one of Candide's moments of greatest isolation. He has lost Pangloss and Cunégonde. Later on, even when those two are absent, Cacambo or Martin will be there almost throughout as companions. But despite his solitariness, he enjoys one ironic consolation: the mental presence of Pangloss's teaching. For in these early chapters Candide carries with him the total imprint of Panglossian thinking. As he tells the Protestant minister in Holland: "There is no effect without cause . . . everything is necessarily linked together, and arranged for the best. It was necessary that I be chased away from Mademoiselle Cunégonde's company, that I run the gauntlet, and it is necessary that I beg for my bread until I am able to earn it; all that could not be otherwise" (127–28). The philosophic master could not have put it better. So far, the callousness of the Baron in kicking him out of the castle, the trickery of the recruiting officers, the personal horrors of his military punishment, and the more general horrors of the battle—none of this has as yet disturbed his faith any more than it would have done that of Pangloss.

But when he is reunited with Pangloss, he begins to ask questions of his mentor. By now his outlook has become darker, for he has been told by Pangloss of Cunégonde's violent death. Besides, he has been appalled at the sight of Pangloss, ravaged by the effects of venereal disease. So he queries, however tentatively, the doctrine of optimism. How, he asks Pangloss, could that beautiful cause, love, have been able to produce in the latter such an abominable effect? And as we have already seen above, Candide wonders whether the Devil is not at the bottom of all this. The seeds of doubt are already there.

Candide, however, is not just a naïvely idealistic young man. On the contrary. When Pangloss has finished his outburst of philo sophical justification for the existence of venereal disease, Candide replies: "That is marvelous . . . but we must get you restored to health" (132). This response exactly anticipates his final remark in the *conte*, in its form as in its attitude: theorizing is all very well, but practical matters must come first. This close parallel with the ending, coming as it does so early in the tale, shows that Candide is already well on the way to an understanding of the true values to be observed in living. Indeed, he demonstrates that he has the practical ability to match his good sense, for he goes to Jacques and paints "such a touching picture of the state to which his friend was reduced" (132) that Jacques is immediately persuaded to help Pangloss. The same desire to be of practical assistance governs Candide's wish, frustrated by Pangloss, to save Jacques from drowning in Lisbon harbor. He is no longer as seduced as he was by the philosopher's reasoning. When the latter develops a theory about the "trail of sulphur" from Peru to Portugal that accounts for earthquakes, Candide merely replies politely, "Nothing is more likely" (136), to the annoyance of Pangloss, who expects assent to what he regards as demonstrative proof. But by now, it is clear, Candide no longer sees as infallible a man who let Jacques die and who prefers to theorize about earthquakes instead of attending his wounds and bringing him the oil and wine for which he has been begging his mentor.

Pangloss fades from the picture, and Candide is once more, briefly, on his own and in a piteous state after the auto-da-fé. His philosophic doubts continue to grow: "If this is the best of all possible worlds, what then are the others?" (139). Yet Pangloss is still respected; he is still "the greatest of philosophers." The progress toward total emancipation will be slow and hesitant.

There now comes the moment when Cunégonde rises, as it were, from the dead. The spell is, however, quickly broken. The choleric Don Issachar appears and Candide has no choice but to kill him in self-defense. A moment later the train of events leads to the equally inevitable murder of the Inquisitor.

This is a decisive moment in Candide's development. First, one needs to note the totally efficacious way in which Candide dispatches both adversaries. Neither has a chance to recover; one sword thrust is enough in each case. This is no accident. Candide's skill is the result of his military training with the Bulgar army, where he had, before deciding to desert, made such remarkable progress that he was "looked upon by his comrades as a prodigy" (123). This prowess at arms is shortly to be demonstrated at Cadiz "with so much grace, rapidity, skill, pride, agility" (151) that he is immediately promoted to captain of an infantry company. Clearly, we have here no gangling youth but a highly trained soldier, with the concomitant capacity to kill unhesitatingly. He has also the psychological toughness to go with it. Whereas Don Issachar is killed in self-defense, the dispatch of the Inquisitor is not so straightforward. The Inquisitor does not have the time to present any threat; he does not get beyond the stage of being a potential menace. Voltaire recounts what thoughts passed through Candide's head: "If this holy man calls for help, he will infallibly have me burned, he could do the same to Cunégonde; he has had me beaten pitilessly; he is my rival; I am implicated in murder, there is not a moment to lose." "This reasoning," adds the narrator, was "clear and prompt" (148–49). To think is to act. Nor does Candide express any remorse, even when Cunégonde shows her horrified bewilderment that he "who was born so gentle" could commit two murders in two minutes. He has, he claims, been drawn into vice by the privations he has had to endure: "When you are in love, jealous, and beaten by the Inquisition, you don't recognize yourself any more" (149).

So any suggestion that Candide is still an innocent must be firmly resisted. He has become a murderer, however justifiable the circumstances; shortly afterwards he volunteers to fight the Jesuit fathers of Paraguay and proves by his military exercises that he has the ability for it. Candide may have deserted twice over from the Bulgars, but the experience he gained in that army has hardened his sensibilities. One might almost paraphrase Cunégonde's remark: "A person of honor may be raped once, but her virtue is strengthened by it."[7] Through the atrocities visited upon them, both she and Candide have learned the art of survival.

Nevertheless, Candide's development in savoir-faire is paradoxical. For it is accompanied by a continuing naïveté on the level of abstract reflection. In the brief interval after the first of the two murders, Candide wonders what Pangloss would have advised, "for he was a great philosopher." Yet when the door flies open to admit the Inquisitor and danger is imminent, Candide immediately demonstrates that he can take care of himself. Practical action proves more efficacious than reliance on philosophic counsels. The same juxtaposition occurs in the following chapter. As a soldier, he is thoroughly capable. As a thinker, he is still far from completely trained. He greets the prospect of the New World with enthusiasm: " 'We are going into another universe,' said Candide, 'that is, doubtless, the one where all is well. For it must be confessed that one might bemoan a little what happens in our own world in physical and moral matters' "(151). This argument contains an inherent fallacy. The disappointments of the Old World in no way justify the conclusion that therefore it will be different in the New—as they are to discover. But Candide hopes rather more than he thinks. He already finds comfort from observing that the Atlantic Ocean is calmer than "the seas of our Europe" (151). It must have been an unusually quiet crossing!

At least, however, the emancipation from Westphalia is complete, now that it has been totally ravaged and no longer contains Cunégonde. In Paraguay, when talking to the young Baron, he refers to it as "the filthy province of Westphalia" (171), a gratuitous comment hardly called for by the circumstances. But Pangloss and Westphalia are not identical. The momentary interruption of misfortunes, when the two Westphalians discover each other, still finds Candide immediately harking back to Pangloss, who would have been, he says, very happy at the encounter. One might add the observation that Pangloss's joy would not have lasted long; Candide's announcement that he is to marry Cunégonde precipitates the fight in which, once again, he has the sword skill to triumph. Here too Candide demonstrates that he is not someone to trifle with in such a situation. There is nothing tentative about the blow he gives the Baron: "In an instant Candide drew his own [sword] and plunged it in the Jesuit Baron's stomach, right up to the hilt" (175). Having committed this brutal act, he begins to weep at how he, "the best man in the world," could have killed three men. Here again the discrepancy between the savagely simple action and the ambivalent thinking is evident. Candide has not yet discovered that human nature, far from being some kind of unchanging datum, is molded by circumstances. He prefers to think that "goodness" is a fixed quality, which one possesses or not as the case may be. While the reader may feel some compassion for

Candide's unfortunate plight in being obliged to kill out of self-defense, that sympathy must be held firmly in check when he can immediately announce himself, with the blood of three men on his hands, as peerless in virtue. The comic effect is quickly heightened by his mock-tragic speech after he and Cacambo make their escape: " 'How can you,' said Candide, 'want me to eat ham. . . . And what will the *Trévoux Journal* say?' " (176).[8] This bathetic reference to the Jesuit paper (one of Voltaire's common satiric targets) removes all dignity from Candide's expressions of grief, as numerous commentators on the *conte* have made clear.

The same naïveté will continue a short time after, when our hero kills the monkeys who are the girls' lovers. Yet once more he demonstrates the same paradoxical mix of personal qualities. The professional killer is again in action. Voltaire remarks that his ability at shooting is such that "he could have shot a hazel-nut off a bush without touching the leaves." Two shots are quite enough to finish off the two monkeys. Yet he believes that this time he is doing good by saving the girls' lives; even better, he foresees rewards for his action: "They are perhaps two young ladies of rank, and this adventure may procure us great advantages in this country" (177). His ingenuousness in failing to recognize a loving relationship between the animals and the girls is matched only by his optimistic delusion that the latter are of noble descent. We are not told by what logic he manages to persuade himself of this cheerful conclusion, especially given that both girls are stark naked.

Candide is struck dumb with disbelief when he learns the truth. This naïve surprise is entirely typical of him; as Cacambo tells him, "You are always astonished at everything." He is still inclined to think, like Pangloss, in rigid categories: animals and human beings *cannot* have a sexual relationship. A priori assumptions dominate. So too when he and Cacambo are captured by the Oreillons and await being thrown into the cooking pot. He urges Cacambo to tell them that it is inhuman to cook human beings (as well as un-Christian). Cannibalism worried Voltaire greatly, and he would in later years try hard to rationalize it by motives such as the lack of good food, or the belief that victors have the right of life and death over the vanquished (Moland, 26:82). So Candide is not wholly mistaken to denounce the inhumanity of the practice as such. The comedy of his protest lies first of all in linking the wider appeal to humanity with the particular invocation of Christianity, as though these naked pagan savages were likely to be deterred by Christian doctrine, and also in making any such appeal at all. The worldly Cacambo instead, as we have seen, finds a more effective device in convincing the Oreillons that they will not, as they had hoped, be "eating Jesuit." Once the savages are persuaded of this truth and begin to treat their prisoners generously, Candide is filled with wonderment all over again, this time at the sudden change in the Oreillons' attitudes. His disposition is, as usual, to flee to generalizations: "After all, pure nature is good, since these people, instead of eating me, did me a thousand courtesies once they knew that I wasn't a Jesuit" (181).[9] The discrepancy between the specific phenomenon and the larger conclusions drawn from it is once again blatant.

So on to Eldorado, where Candide's ingenuous wonderment is, exceptionally, matched by Cacambo. But here too it is Candide alone who seeks to make sense of the place in relation to Panglossianism. At least one certain truth emerges from this new experience: whatever else, Westphalia is now definitively shown to be less than the best possible place in the world. Even Pangloss, concludes Candide, would have had to admit the superiority of Eldorado. Our hero is right about the educative effects of travel; but he still retains a simplistic view of Pangloss in thinking that the discovery of new places would have done anything to change his master's outlook. The memory of Pangloss as a fine philosopher continues to live on in Candide's mind. The realization that Pangloss is unteachable and merely absorbs every new experience to fit in with his theories has not yet penetrated.

But they must leave this marvelous place. Cunégonde is not there, and besides, Candide and Cacambo are only on the same footing as everyone else, whereas in the outside world the riches of Eldorado will make them wealthier than "all the kings put together" and give them security against all Inquisitors. Candide may be sentimental about Cunégonde, and he is still naïve enough to imagine that wealth will cure all their woes, but he has learned that wealth gives comparative ease and security in the world. Voltaire had made this discovery in his own life, as demonstrated by a striking phrase in his *Mémoires* (1759): "In France you have to be hammer or anvil; I had been born anvil" (Moland, 1:44). The only way to become independent, he goes on, is to acquire one's own fortune.

So it might be better to see Candide's decision as a step on the road to greater wisdom rather than yet another act of outright folly. The king of Eldorado, it is true, tells the pair that they are foolish to leave and that "when you are fairly comfortable somewhere or other, you should stay there" (192),[10] advice that will, by the end of the *conte*, prove invaluable. But ordinary human beings are not made for Eldorado. Candide may be led on by a mixture of foolish nostalgia for Cunégonde and grubby acquisitiveness. On the latter count, however, he is beginning to be less "candide."

Having left Eldorado, the pair encounter the black slave outside Surinam. It is here, contemplating the slave's misery, that Candide announces his break with Pangloss: " 'O Pangloss!' cried Candide, 'you had not guessed at this abomination; it is finished, I must at last renounce your optimism.' " And when Cacambo asks him to define "optimism," he comes out with the famous remark: "It is the mania for asserting that all is well when one is not" (196).[11]

But, as we have already noted, the black slave episode is an interpolation, and not entirely a happy one. Candide speaks out for Voltaire on optimism as nowhere else, a stance that somewhat detracts from the narrative subtlety of his portrayal. Nor does this mark the definitive abandonment of Pangloss's philosophy, a discrepancy that the author may have overlooked. (In any event, when Candide later slips back into a measure of agreement with Pangloss, the effect of his righteous anger here is rather undermined.) As before, it would be best to see this episode as an eloquent passage in its own right rather than as an integral part of the *conte*.

With Cacambo's departure we enter upon a more somber period in Candide's life. Martin is about to succeed Cacambo as companion; where Cacambo had always sought to be cheerful and enterprising, Martin is gloomy and fatalistic. The darker mood is heralded, before Martin's arrival, by Vanderdendur's treachery, followed by the judge's mercenary conduct. Candide's morale reaches one of its lowest points in the tale: "The wickedness of men presented itself to him in all its ugliness, sad thoughts alone preoccupied his mind" (199). This gloom precipitates him into actively seeking an unhappy companion for his return voyage to Europe.

The change in Candide's mood is remarkable. He who has always tried to discover the silver lining to every cloud now wishes to listen to nothing but tales of misery. Once again, Candide wishes that Pangloss were present; but the attitude is now much more detached. As he condescendingly puts it, "That Pangloss would be hard put to it to prove his system" (200). Only in Eldorado does all go well. For the moment, not even the place where Cunégonde is living can be exempted from the general condemnation.

So the stage is set for confronting this temporarily pessimistic Candide with the arch-pessimist Martin. It is not long, however, before the difference between them is apparent. Candide begins to recover from his fit of gloom and to realize that he is still well off. Besides, unlike Martin, he retains that precious faculty, hope; for Cunégonde is still the object of his quest. So it is that Panglossian optimism creeps insidiously back in from time to time—"especially at the end of the meal" (201), notes Voltaire with incisive irony. As we have already observed, food and wine can operate a remarkably tonic effect upon even the most despairing of moods. Candide begins to dispute with Martin. He interprets as a favorable omen the return of his lost sheep and prefers to see the hand of divine justice in Vanderdendur's death, leaving out of account the hundred others who died innocently with him. Even so, the malice in human nature continues to perplex him, and he is now, in Martin's company, of a decidedly more reflective frame of mind. Have men, he asks, always been wicked? Here Voltaire indulges him with a bravura display of 19 different adjectives to make the point. Yet, confronted with Martin's totally negative views on the subject, he still clings vaguely to free will. As he makes clear later over dinner in Paris, the evil in the world is caused by human beings; but this time he adds that "they cannot help it" (217)—a total contradiction of his previous profession of human liberty, which only serves to point up the confusion in his thinking.

Now comes a potentially distressing moment in Candide's life: he is seduced into being unfaithful to Cunégonde. (One has to infer that when he was offered girls by the Oreillons, he had refused the temptation, for the experience left no impression upon him that we hear about.) But despite his yearning for his beloved and desire to be in her arms, the infidelity does not seem to be particularly traumatic; Candide merely feels "some remorse" (218) and determines to ask her forgiveness when he at last finds her.[12] In the meantime, he continues as naïvely as ever in Paris: not only is he robbed and swindled at cards, but he is tricked at least for a while into believing that he has rediscovered Cunégonde in the French capital, against all the odds. Only by bribery does he avoid imprisonment. Once freed, he learns about Damiens's attempt upon the king's life as a result of religious fanaticism and breaks out into fulminations upon the awful things that take place in France: " 'Ah, the monsters,' cried Candide, 'what! such horrors among a people who sing and dance! Can I not escape as quickly as possible from this land where monkeys provoke tigers?' " (221). It is noteworthy that this outburst, conveying Voltaire's own sentiments,[13] occurs in the final emendations to the text before the first edition. As with the black slave episode, the author clearly felt the need in his last revisions to give Candide a more forceful role. This would appear to be further proof that Voltaire did not intend his hero to function as just a fool until the narrator operated a simple reversal of character in the final chapter. The evolution of Candide is more subtle and more gradual.

For the hero has certainly inclined by now to a disenchanted view of human nature. When he and Martin set sail for England, he wishes to know if people are as mad over there as in France. At the sight of Byng's execution, he might as well be uttering Martin's thoughts when he asks: "What devil is it that holds sway throughout the world?" It is Candide who makes the commonsensical observation that "the French admiral was as far from the English admiral as the other way round" (224). He is still learning about the world but is now equipped with a sense of judgment that was previously lacking. His reactions, too, are being taken more seriously by the narrator. If he and Martin do not set foot on English soil, it is because "Candide was so bewildered and shocked by what he saw" (224) that he refuses even this fleeting encounter. The chillingly simple way in which Voltaire recounts Byng's execution encourages the reader to participate in that bewilderment and shock. The Venetian experience only adds to Candide's despairing mood, when he fails to find Cacambo and Cunégonde. He regrets having left Eldorado. He is convinced that Cunégonde is dead and that nothing but death remains for him. He explicitly agrees with Martin when the latter states that "the whole world is naught but illusion and calamity" (225). He loses all zest for life and refuses to take any part in the amusements of the carnival. Martin at this point has all the good lines, with Candide bereft of his usual hopefulness. Then Giroflée and Paquette turn up. Candide seizes on their cheerful appearance as one exception to the general misery. But their story quickly forces him to admit that Martin is right in judging them also to be unhappy creatures.

Yet hope never totally dies in Candide's breast. They have met Paquette again; he sees it as a good omen for rediscovering Cunégonde. He wants to believe that the gondoliers are content because they are always singing, or that Pococuranté is the happiest of men because he disdains his possessions. Martin wins every one of these arguments. But Candide's rediscovered joy in life, when he recovers from the terrible disappointment on arriving in Venice and failing to find Cacambo, is irrepressible. If no one else in the whole world is happy, he says, at least he is, because he lives in hopes of seeing Cunégonde again. Martin's reaction to this naïve fantasy is characteristically slighting.

As we have seen, this time it turns out that Candide is closer to the truth. One could hardly construct a less logical inference than that, because he has met Paquette again, he will also find Cunégonde. But in the world of *Candide* reality ignores logic. He *is* about to see Cunégonde again; Cacambo *does* reappear; hope still has a valid place. The world should not be given over to pure boredom and despair. Candide will go on yet again to reveal his ingenuousness about Pococuranté. It nevertheless remains true that our hero, who can still admire the beauty of Pococuranté's mistresses, the Raphael pictures, the music being played, who appreciates Homer, Virgil, Horace, Cicero, and Milton, has a broadly saner view of things than the blasé Venetian senator.

The education that Candide has been receiving ever since Eldorado is almost at an end. He has yet to see at first hand the emptiness of worldly power in the spectacle of the six kings. But although no longer as naïve as he was, he is still given to reiterating that Pangloss was right. Even the news from Cacambo that Cunégonde has become horribly ugly does not shake him. It is a pity, he says; but it is his duty to love her forever. The reality of her lost beauty has not yet sunk in.

The scales are, however, about to fall from his eyes. The sight of Cunégonde puts a sudden end to the long quest for the beloved object, and she will soon reveal that she is as ill natured as she is ugly. Any further fantasy of an erotic kind has to founder on the reality presented before his eyes. Pangloss has been similarly reduced from the plane of the ideal. Now he is seen in his true colors, as the inflexible character who tells Candide that his own terrible sufferings will not make the slightest difference to his first belief in Leibniz, from which he will never stray.

The little band has been gathered together at last. The time has come for a final reckoning. Faith in impossibly beautiful principles and people has been wholly confounded. But the immediate reality is for the moment only boredom and despair.

Candide has already demonstrated his generosity in purchasing the freedom of his companions. It is typical of his sympathetic disposition that his eye is caught by Pangloss and the Baron on the galley because they are rowing so badly and therefore being punished more than the rest. He approaches them in the first place out of pity. Now, finally, the time has come to harness his best qualities to useful ends. Aided by the negative counsels of the dervish and the more positive example of the Turkish farmer, Candide "reflected deeply" (258) on the latter's remarks. There will be no more naïve questings, no more dependence upon the counsels of Pangloss, the Old Woman, Cacambo, Martin—all of whom have taught him, by positive or negative precept and example, about the world. Whatever the future may hold, however fragile the security of the garden, so long as it survives he will take the lead in cultivating it. His education complete, he is his own master at last.

7

Structure and Form

It is commonly said that *Candide* is a loosely constructed, episodic work. To be sure, Voltaire was much given to composing the brief article, and there are innumerable examples in his *Dictionnaire philosophique* (1764) or his polemical works. In other *contes*, such as *Zadig*, *Micromégas*, and *L'Ingénu*, the chapters are usually quite short. So too in *Candide*, where at least half the chapters are under 1,000 words or barely exceed that number. Some, like chapters 23 (the Byng episode) and 29 (Candide's discovery of Cunégonde's ugliness), are under 500 words, while yet remaining among the most powerful in the story. Apart from the Paris chapter, which is almost double the length of any other, none exceeds about 2,000 words. *Candide* runs to under 15,000 words; Voltaire has divided up what is, in terms of length, only a long short story into no fewer than 30 chapters. There would therefore seem to be a case for arguing that the tale is bitty and fragmented.

We shall consider later to what extent there is discontinuity in *Candide*. Before doing so, however, we should not settle too easily for a belief that the tale, for all its apparent randomness of event, lacks a unifying structure. First of all, it has a geographical shape that matches the progress of the plot. Candide starts out in the Old World, which is revealed to be full of misery and injustice. He flees to the New World, which, Eldorado apart, turns out to be as bad, returns to the Old in a new guise because he is now a man of wealth, and at last settles in a country that is on the margins of Europe. Within this global voyage, Eldorado is given a special place, almost exactly halfway through; it is possible to read *Candide* as a two-act drama with Eldorado as the entr'acte. One may also argue that the 30 chapters observe a ternary form: the first 10, "Europe I," see Candide through and out of Europe; chapters 11–20, "America," deal with America and the two transatlantic voyages (after the Old Woman's tale on board ship, which takes up the first two chapters); and the final 10, "Europe II," begin with Candide in sight of France and take him and Martin once again through and eventually out of Europe. There is certainly symmetry here. But it is somewhat abstract, depending upon chapter units rather than plot development, and as we noted, it requires the rather artificial inclusion of the Old Woman's tale in the American section. Besides, the average length of chapters increases, generally speaking, in the second 15, so that the blocks "Europe I," "America," and "Europe II" are by no means equal in size.

Various other structural patterns have been proposed, some more artificial and less useful than others. Perhaps the most helpful for an understanding of the story relates to Candide's companions. For the latter have their exits and their entrances carefully orchestrated. Only Candide is present in every chapter (albeit occasionally just as an audience to someone else's narrative), and he is only on rare occasions left on his own without someone to talk to. If then we look at the *conte* in this light, a clear line of development emerges.

The first section belongs to Pangloss, even though he is not present throughout it. He impregnates Candide with his values, which the latter has quickly to reassess in the light of brutal experience once he is kicked out of Eden. In these early chapters he encounters, at first or second hand, the phenomena of war, syphilis, and earthquake, three of the most devastating disasters in human experience. To these are added the gratuitousness of the auto-da-fé, whose horror is equaled only by its absurdity as a means of placating Providence. Candide, for his part, is beaten up twice by the time Cunégonde reappears. Voltaire stresses right away, once out of Westphalia, the various terrible experiences that obtain in the real world, so as to demolish from the start the falsity of Panglossian optimism.

The Inquisition effectively removes Pangloss from the stage until the closing section. His teachings linger on in Candide's mind, but Voltaire has by now begun to show up his ineffectuality. The appearance of the Old Woman at the end of chapter 6 inaugurates a period dominated by Cunégonde's presence in Candide's life. The return of his beloved signifies a momentary pause in the onslaught on Candide, while she tells her tale, followed by the Old Woman's. Here we discover a more specific reality: what man does to woman in a time of anarchy. Physically the weaker sex and an object of sexual desire, she must serve whatever needs her male captors require of her. However, Cunégonde has not only survived the atrocities committed upon her but even achieved a modus vivendi, however fragile. Not all women are so fortunate. The Old Woman must provide her own narrative explicitly to show, as she herself says, that women's sufferings can be much, much worse. Like Cunégonde, she has known what it is to be a sexual chattel, albeit with greater physical humiliations. In addition, she has witnessed the murder of her fiancé at the wedding feast, she has been betrayed by the Italian in whom she had put her trust, and she has suffered to the point of absurdity the horrible excision of a buttock. The awfulness of her tale permits Voltaire to introduce a more profound theme, on the meaningfulness of life. We have seen how her comments on suicide reach to the heart of *Candide* and its significance.

Cunégonde, with the powerful assistance of the Old Woman, has served her purpose. The arrival in Buenos Aires announces a renewal of Candide's misfortunes, and by the end of chapter 13 he must flee once more. Bereft of his beloved, he has nonetheless acquired a new companion, Cacambo, who will dominate the New World section where he acts as Candide's guide and safekeeper through America. Here at last is a true and loyal mentor of sorts, at least where pragmatic matters are concerned. It is he who, when they have run the gamut of what the New World has to offer, justifiably sums it up for Candide: "You can see . . . that this hemisphere is no better than the other one" (182). Candide lives dangerously in this unfamiliar environment and twice comes close to death. But in this section the emphasis is much more firmly placed on absurdity than on danger. Voltaire, having comprehensively shown how cruel and heartless human behavior can be, is now intent on demonstrating that it can also be quite bizarre, even comically so. In Paraguay, for instance, the Jesuits wage war upon the kings of Spain and Portugal, while in Europe they act as confessors to these selfsame monarchs. The Baron himself is an exemplary case of such inconsequence, totally refusing to sanction Candide's marriage to Cunégonde despite the fact that his aristocratic snobbery has not the slightest relevance to any of their present situations. Shortly after, we discover from the Oreillons that it is possible for women to take monkeys as lovers, however curious that may seem to the reader, as it does to Candide. But the potential horrors of cannibalism are played down and reduced to the comic phrase that amused Voltaire's contemporaries: "Let us eat Jesuit" (179).

It is therefore fitting that the spectacle of such a topsy-turvy world should lead up to the strangest place of all in *Candide:* Eldorado. We have already seen that Voltaire uses Eldorado to point to certain values, but that the total meaning of the *conte* does not reside here. It is a resting place from the world's evils; it contributes to Candide's education; but it is not a place in which to stay. This is, as it were, the true New World, quite different from our corrupt way of life but ultimately unfit for human beings. However, its influence will be felt throughout the rest of the story, partly because Candide now knows of a certainty that Westphalia is not the best possible place in the world, but also because his way of life is assured against constant threats of poverty and starvation by the treasures he has brought out of Eldorado. He will no longer need the quick wits of Cacambo. With the emergence of the pair from Eldorado, Cacambo's special contribution is virtually at an end. A new order is about to begin, requiring a different kind of dialogue. The American experience, too, is virtually complete, save for the treachery of Vanderdendur (which could as easily have happened anywhere else in the world, as *Candide* has sufficiently made clear) and the episode of the black slave, itself a late interpolation.

Cacambo leaves Candide to rescue Cunégonde. Candide, left on his own, sinks into despair at the foul play of Vanderdendur and the chicanery of the law courts. He now requires a darker kind of temperament than Cacambo's to suit his black mood. Enter Martin, the last of his companions. The stage is set for a new testing of philosophic attitudes in the light of experience; but now the worldview on display is pessimism, which is not so easily disposed of as Pangloss's complacency. The naval battle in which Vanderdendur perishes is accompanied by a commentary from Martin that matches the terrible massacre (whereas the earlier land battle involving Candide had simply been recounted without the addition of observations by any character, Candide included). Martin's Manichean outlook will easily accommodate the frenetic sham world of Paris, the lunacies of the English (who are, he says, suffering from "a different kind of madness" [223]), the secret unhappiness of Paquette and Giroflée, the ennui of Pococuranté. For the space of several chapters Martin holds sway, Candide sometimes falling under his spell when he turns to Martin in his inquiries about the nature of things. But his limitations are decisively shown up when Cacambo reappears, contrary to Martin's confident predictions, and it becomes clear that he is no more in possession of a complete truth about the universe than anyone else.

So Martin's special role is at an end as the story transfers from Venice to Constantinople. Candide sounds him out for the last time on board ship about human unhappiness, to which Martin returns a characteristically gloomy answer. But the inquiry on which Candide had embarked with him is over. With the reemergence of Cunégonde the time has come for action. The structure of the *conte* is no longer based on a link between Candide and one or two others. He now finds himself liberating and leading a whole little community. Dismayed by Cunégonde, freed of the philosophic illusions purveyed by Pangloss and Martin, he is ready to absorb the advice of the dervish and the Turkish farmer and to put it to practical use. Candide no longer looks to any of his previous mentors. They all take their places around him. Voltaire has by now tried out a whole series of approaches and found them all wanting.

But if one were to talk only of the structural unity of *Candide* the impression left would be a distorted one. In this tale, it is the incoherence of things that is above all made manifest. Voltaire's attack is directed precisely at a metaphysical system of order in which everything has its place, in which a "great chain of being" accounts for the whole cosmos, in which causality can explain all things, if need be ever since the beginning of the world. The author replaces this vision, at first apparently consoling but ultimately destructive of all human initiative, with a harsher picture. The way the world acts, in particular the way human beings behave, defies rational understanding. Martin's Manichean system, because it too seeks to impose a transcendental pattern, is likewise proved fallible. In *Candide* teleological meanings are replaced by the aleatory. So far as Candide is concerned, it is chance that presides over the succession of happenings.

Even so, the *conte* must not be seen as a forerunner of the "absurd" in modern fiction. Candide's world is full of ridiculous and meaningless elements, but human beings are not totally deprived of the ability tomake sense out of it. As we have noted before, the dervish's little parable must be given its full weight. To the mice in the hold of the ship, the journey to Egypt makes no sense, and the Highness who decreed the journey pays them no attention whatsoever. But the ship is going somewhere, as the result of some obscure purpose. A cosmic harmony prevails; Newton's sublime discovery of the law of gravitation was for Voltaire the unshakable demonstration of it. Within that general arrangement, human beings have a function, as the ending of *Candide* or the lessons of Eldorado show. The good qualities of Jacques and Cacambo are intermingled with the evil Inquisitors or Vanderdendur. As we have seen before, Voltaire's vision is binary.

How then to portray it? Rational argument alone would not have made a masterpiece out of *Candide*. The Leibnizian system is demolished in its stead by, as René Pomeau puts it, "the obsession with a style."[1] Style alone can convey the dual complexity. The tale must contain horrors. But it must also be resolutely comic; pathos or tragedy must be assiduously avoided. Since *Candide* is a tale about life and survival, death plays little part in it. Voltaire is totally indifferent to the notion that preparation for death and contemplation of it may bring dignity to a life. The "deaths" of Pangloss, Cunégonde, and the young Baron turn out to be false, permitting farcically miraculous recoveries in each case. When death actually occurs, it is peremptory, leaving no room for the flights of the human spirit. Jacques is dispatched in a trice; a sort of cosmic shrug of total indifference is shown by all save Candide. The death of Admiral Byng, which Voltaire had in reality made unavailing attempts to prevent by intervening in Byng's court-martial, becomes a black joke: "While chatting in this way they [Candide and Martin] arrived in Portsmouth: a crowd was covering the shore, paying close attention to a rather fat man who was kneeling, his eyes blindfolded, on the deck of one of the fleet's vessels; four soldiers, who had taken up their positions opposite this man, each fired three bullets into his skull, in the most peaceful manner imaginable, and the whole assembly went home feeling extremely satisfied" (223–24). Note the use here, as so often in *Candide,* of plain numbers for effect. An unjust and doubtless bloody death is reduced to an exercise in arithmetic. Each soldier dispatches his three bullets as neatly as if he were putting them into a box to make up a round dozen. Regimental order rules. Hence the paradox that a military execution is carried out "peacefully," and the further sardonic irony that the mob was "satisfied" by this entertainment. Here is no room for tears. Byng is effectively distanced from us as "a rather fat man"; the mock-pedantic "rather" adds to the horror comedy.

To capture the tone he requires, Voltaire has recourse to parody. No single model serves, but intertextual echoes abound. For instance, Fénelon's didactic novel *Télémaque* (1699), widely read throughout the eighteenth century, can be discerned behind Candide's adventures. The hero Télémaque, like Candide, is on a quest. But whereas the former enjoys the benefit of his ever-wise guide-mentor, Candide learns fitfully, and often by negative example, from those who proffer him advice. Heroic romances like Prévost's *Manon Lescaut* also play their part. For *Manon* conveys precisely that sense of fatal destiny (whether or not the hero, des Grieux, is deemed to be a credible narrator) that Voltaire is eager to disrupt. Manon's beauty, even in death, is proof against all degradation. The contrast with the raddled, sour Cunégonde is all too obvious. A more subtle parallel may, however, be found in earlier passages from both novels. Des Grieux has been separated from Manon and, as he thought, has recovered from his passion for her, when she unexpectedly reenters his life: "Lord! what a surprising apparition! . . . It was she, but more lovable and brilliant than I had ever seen her. . . . Her whole face appeared to me an enchantment."[2] The moment when the Old Woman leads Candide to rediscover Cunégonde, whom he thinks dead, bears some resemblances: "What a moment! what a surprise! he believes he is seeing Mademoiselle Cunégonde; he was, indeed, seeing her, it was she herself" (142). What was sublime in *Manon* has become the stuff of comic banality ("what a surprise!"). The stage is set for Cunégonde to tell Candide that, yes, she *was* raped and her stomach *was* split open by a sword; "but one doesn't always die from these two accidents" (142).

Prevost makes eloquent use of the first-person narrative to describe the effect of Manon's reappearance upon des Grieux; we share directly with des Grieux what he feels. Voltaire, by contrast, employs the third-person authorial technique, with equally devastating but totally different results. For he separates reader from character, interposing himself: "He believes he is seeing . . . he was, indeed, seeing her." It is as if one were looking through the wrong end of a telescope at the slightly ridiculous reactions of our hero. Des Grieux is struck dumb by an overpowering vision; Candide, on the other hand, is simply bewildered. From beginning to end in *Candide*, the authorial presence is unremitting. Candide may be onstage the whole time, but behind him ever looms the narrator. From the very first words we are told what to think: "There was in Westphalia, in the castle of the Baron of Thunder-ten-tronckh, a young boy on whom nature had conferred the sweetest manners. His physiognomy revealed his soul. He had quite a good sense of judgment, along with the simplest of minds; that is why, I believe, he was called Candide" (118). Compare this with the beginning of Voltaire's *Zadig:* "In the time of King Moabdar there was in Babylon a young man called Zadig, born with a fine natural disposition that had been strengthened by education. Although rich and young, he knew how to temper his passions; he was never affected; he did not wish to be always right, and he knew how to respect men's weaknesses."[3] Though he has much to learn about human malice, Zadig is a conventional hero from the start. But Candide is right away placed at a remove. As with Byng's execution, the word *assez* ("quite a good sense") is subversive. Candide may have a promising sweetness of nature, but we are invited immediately to beware of his capacity for judgment and his simple soul.

This comparison with *Zadig* shows that Voltaire is ready to parody his own works as much as those of others. In *Zadig* as in *Candide* the opening sentence contains *il y avait*; the same is also true of Voltaire's *Micromégas*, like Zadig a forerunner of *Candide*. In *Candide* the phrase *il y avait* is give pride of place as the very opening of the *conte*, the author seeking to exploit full value from the fairy-tale atmosphere of "once upon a time" before rudely shattering it in the very next phrase with the wholly unromantic name of Thunder-ten-tronckh.

Parody permits of a whole range of hyperbolic devices. Voltaire indulges himself in superlatives, for instance, when the occasion warrants it. Once again, the opening chapter will serve well as a case in point. Everything in Thunder-ten-tronckh's garden is lovely, or at least appears to be. The Baron is "one of the most powerful lords in Westphalia" (118). His wife has acquired "very considerable esteem" (119) (but because she is very fat!). The chambermaid is "very pretty and very docile" (120). Cunégonde, after witnessing the sexual encounter between her and Pangloss, is "all agitated, all pensive, all full of the desire to be well informed" (120). Candide kisses her hand with "a quite special graciousness" (120). The reason for these high-flown descriptions is already clear; in the fourth paragraph of the tale Pangloss announces that this is "the best of all possible worlds" (119). This is because the Baron's château "had a door and windows" (118). As we have seen, the dogs running about the yards become a hunting pack when it serves his purpose; the village curate is promoted to the Baron's Grand Almoner. Everything in the château is based on sham except for sexual desire and the brutality of Candide's expulsion. Even the pretty, docile maid turns out later to have infected Pangloss with venereal disease. Reality quickly destroys this façade of pretense and ostentation when Candide is ejected. The word *all* returns to close out the chapter and give ironic counterpoint to the earlier romantic sentiments: "And all was consternation in the finest and most agreeable of all possible châteaus" (121).

Here is a typical example of mixed registers: a smoothly classical style, full of bland compliments, masks a profoundly satiric intent. Similarly, characters are given enough rope, through their own utterances, to hang themselves. Pangloss, for example, definitively establishes the madness of his philosophy in that first chapter when he argues the finality of all things by pointing out that legs were made for breeches and that noses were made to hang spectacles on. But Pangloss is an easy target. Voltaire's treatment of Candide needs to be more subtle if Candide is to retain any credibility in the denouement. After the atrocities of the auto-da-fé, we witness his total distress: "terrified, dumbfounded, distraught, all bloody, all palpitating" (139). Voltaire goes on to report his anguished soliloquy: "If this is the best of all possible worlds, what then are the others? . . . Oh my dear Pangloss, the greatest of philosophers, did I have to see you hanged without knowing why! Oh my dear Anabaptist! the best of men, did you have to be drowned in the harbor! Oh Mademoiselle Cunégonde, a treasure among girls, did you have to have your belly split open!" (139–40). The gentle reader who starts out in sympathetic harmony with Candide during this impassioned speech will find himself betrayed before the end. Pangloss has been hanged and that is awful, though one may reserve judgment on "the greatest of philosophers"; Jacques is drowned and that is worse; but the lament for Cunégonde plummets straight into total bathos. In French it is clearer yet, as the monologue highlights the vulgar word *ventre* by ending with it. Besides, Candide lapses into sexual innuendo by his unfortunate remark. The change in tone is disconcerting. Until the last phrase, the language and the phraseology have both been of impeccable classical pedigree: the dignity of the invocations, the descriptions in general and the superlative terms, the inversion (*faut-il*), the purity of language—until we are toppled from the sublime heights into the vulgarity of a slit belly.

The rhetorical effect of the narrative, here as elsewhere, is to deaden sensibility and stimulate the reader's critical awareness. Voltaire is much given to a reductionist technique of false naïveté, where things are voided of their usual connotations and therefore appear as pure phenomena; it had been a favorite weapon in his armory ever since at least the *Lettres philosophiques* 25 years before. The auto-da-fé is an excellent example. This ceremony, once divested of its sense of spiritual atonement to God for human sin, becomes a pure spectacle of ridiculous horror. The designated victims include two Jews, but Voltaire does not name them as Jews. He uses a periphrastic device. They are presented as "two Portuguese who, while eating a chicken, had torn off the bacon" (138). The reader is forced to reflect on this paradox and to consider the appalling injustice visited upon the pair. Once the associations surrounding Jewishness are reduced to a pedantic detail of harmless dietary habits, their essential innocence of any crime and therefore the awful nonsense of putting them to death become overwhelmingly evident, without the need for the author to make a single explicit comment on their behalf.

Similarly disproportionate to the terrible punishment are the offenses of Pangloss and Candide, "the one for having spoken, the other for having listened with an approving air" (139). But once an auto-da-fé has been ordered, the awful majesty of the Inquisition, with its long tradition of colorful ritual, can be given full play. Voltaire chooses to enhance the appalling cruelty of the whole spectacle by indulging in a pedantic description based on careful documentation. He deems it important to point out that "Candide's mitre and cloak were painted with flames reversed and devils without tails and talons; but Pangloss's devils possessed talons and tails and the flames were upright" (139). So too with the extra detail about Pangloss, that his being hanged was contrary to custom. Once again, the significance and purpose of the auto-da-fé are removed and the ceremony reduced to pure formality. In this way, it is less the horror that is stressed, for Voltaire does not go into any of the ghastly details, than the sheer stupidity of such barbarous, magical thinking. To clinch the point, Voltaire ends the paragraph with a statement of devastating simplicity: "That same day, the earth shook again with a terrible thunder" (139).

This brutal fact is set in counterpoint to the reason given, in the preceding paragraph of the text, for the auto-da-fé. The University of Coimbra had decreed it on the basis of an impeccably rationalist assumption, that "the sight of a few people being slowly burned alive, with great pomp and ceremony, is an infallible secret for preventing earthquakes" (138). Here is causality gone mad. Causation, as we have already had occasion to observe, is a prime target of Voltaire's satire. Consider, for instance, the long series of events or names set up repeatedly by Pangloss to explain this or that. Voltaire makes much ironic play with clauses in *Candide*. In particular, his use of the little linking word *car* (for) is frequent and generally insidious. One of the best examples comes, characteristically, from Pangloss offering consolation to the earthquake survivors: " 'For,' he said, 'all this is the best that is possible; for if there is a volcano in Lisbon, it could not be somewhere else. For it is impossible that things should not be where they are. For all is well' " (137). It is a circular argument, demonstrating nothing at all, the *car* series relying ultimately on a blind belief in optimism.

Parody of the conventional novel also extends to the use Voltaire makes of space and time in *Candide*. Places are described in a skeletal way. What, for instance, does the philosopher make of England, a country much praised in earlier works, such as the *Lettres philosophiques*, as the home of liberty, tolerance, philosophy, and science? Here it is given scant treatment. It has become simply a country infected by the lunacy of the Seven Years' War. England is now reduced to Portsmouth harbor and the brutal execution of an admiral unlucky enough to have become a notorious example. Holland, apart from Jacques, is the place where a Protestant minister turns away a starving Candide while his wife pours the slops onto our hero's head. Even where greater attention is paid to cities, such as Paris and Venice, the notations mainly relate to exaggerated social conduct. Paris is the home of treachery, playacting (both literal and metaphorical), and social alienation, and Venice is a carnival for pseudomonarchs. As for Buenos Aires, we know nothing at all about it, except that in it resides a governor possessed of disdainful arrogance and an impossibly pretentious name, with lustful designs upon Cunégonde. This is a world of stylized fantasy, where a few details are brilliantly highlighted to stress the nonsensicality of human behavior.

So too with time. The very considerable amount of chronological detail is merely obfuscatory. It is a sort of jocular camouflage, for in reality this story does not evolve in a consistently linear way. The point has often been made that the reader goes directly from the fine weather of chapter 1, such that Pangloss is able to make love to Paquette out of doors, to the heavy snowfall of chapter 2, and it is always possible that Voltaire did not notice this apparent inconsistency. But whether inconsistent or not (and the Westphalian climate must have been quite capable in the eighteenth century, as it is today, of following a day of mild warmth with one of snow at certain seasons), it matters little. The château of Thunder-ten-tronckh is a "terrestrial paradise" where the sun, at least metaphorically, always shines. The surrounding snowy fields where Candide finds himself after being exiled accord well with the beginning of his personal fall from summer to winter. Thereafter, Voltaire follows Candide's career with many detailed temporal indications. In the period, for instance, leading up to his reunion with Cuné gonde, we know that there is some lapse of time before Candide, now well trained as a soldier, makes up his mind to desert his regiment, since he takes the decision to do so on "a fine spring day" (123). His subsequent punishment takes three weeks to heal, before the battle begins that leads to his flight into Holland. His stay in that country lasts two months, before he leaves for Lisbon. The earthquake and his arrest take just two days; the auto-da-fé occurs a week later; and within a further two days Candide rediscovers Cunégonde. It would seem that something like six months in all has elapsed.

For Cunégonde, however, the time seems to have had other dimensions. Her sufferings at the hands of the Bulgars appear to coincide with Candide's involvement in the battle, for we are told that this military engagement comes at the outbreak of war; the invasion of the château certainly does not precede it. But after that she spends three months with the Bulgar captain, and then at least six months (quite possibly more—there is some indeterminate interval between her being bought by Don Issachar and being spotted "one day" at Mass by the Grand Inquisitor) resisting both her protectors.

How does that square with Candide's two months in Holland and ten days in Lisbon? Not at all, unless one supposes that Candide's wanderings from the battlefield to Holland take him more than six months, an unlikely hypothesis. But this sort of chronological analysis, which might be of some value in, say, a novel by Prévost, is of no relevance here. Time, in the sense of evolution from an irrevocable past into the present, is largely absent from *Candide*. Death as a destiny does not exist. Where there is progression in the *conte*, above all in Candide's development, it is fitful and sometimes even contradictory. Cunégonde does not gradually lose her looks in some gentle aging process: in Buenos Aires she is still desirable, in Turkey her beauty has, quite simply, vanished. It is an action presented by the author as brutally as any other event in the story. Nor does the tale lead inevitably up to a closure in some promised land. Indeed, when the characters settle in the Turkish garden, at first they have no inkling that here is the end of their travels. There is no moment of epiphany to tell them, "This is it." It is up to them to discover, from unpromising surroundings, what can be made of things. The story, it is true, charts Candide's apprenticeship in a general way until he achieves some sort of practical wisdom. To that extent it is a bildungsroman. But the nature of the journey, and the way it is described, make of it more a parody of the genre than an exemplary model of it.

For underneath the overall structure we noted at the outset of this chapter, discontinuity abounds in *Candide*. Voltaire strives throughout to surprise and often to disconcert. The massacre of the Baron Thunder-ten-tronckh's family is recounted variously by Pangloss, Cunégonde, and the Baron's son. Pangloss and Cunégonde agree that her mother was cut to pieces and that Cunégonde was stabbed. But Pangloss, with a capacity for exaggeration well in line with his penchant for fantastic explanations, asserts that she was killed by the stabbing, after "being raped as much as it is possible to be" (13). Cunégonde corrects this version to something less melodramatic: one knife wound, and one rape. Pangloss also recounts the rape of the Baron's son, perhaps more plausibly in view of the latter's homosexual propensities (was this perhaps where he first discovered them?); when the young Baron contributes his own version of the past horrors, he mentions that his sister was raped but fails to add that he was too. Once again, the reader will not expend useless energy in trying to decide who is right. Whether Cunégonde was raped once or often, whether the young Baron was raped at all, makes no difference to the essential fact of man's utter animality in such situations of war when all normal inhibitions have been destroyed.

Here is a case of casual inconsistencies undermining once again the conventions of orthodox narration. Voltaire is equally capable of exaggerating those very devices, not only by comic use of tragic discourse, as we have seen, but also by the use of plot. Coincidence, for example, is exploited with abandon. Characters are forever running into one another over and over, as though the world were a global village. One particularly absurd instance is Pangloss and the Baron finding themselves "in exactly the same galley and on the same bench" (250). Just to add to the similarity, they have received exactly the same punishment for their indiscretions. The Baron recounts: "A cadi [judge] had me given a hundred lashes on the soles of my feet and sentenced me to the galleys" (248). Pangloss undergoes a similar experience: "I was taken to the cadi, who had me given a hundred lashes on the soles of my feet and sent me to the galleys" (250). Very minor differences of language serve only to heighten the identicality in all other respects of these two statements. Why should Voltaire seek here to develop this apparently gratuitous parallel? Probably because he wants once again to satirize the belief in neat order and causation. This hypothesis is strengthened when we find Pangloss, at the end of his account, claiming to Candide that "the chain of events of this universe led you to our galley, and . . . you purchased our ransom" (250). As always for Pangloss, everything has a brighter side.

Variety, too, is a hallmark of Voltaire's style. The rhythm of the narrative never remains constant for long. There are new effects at every turn. Space does not permit a full appraisal of such contrasts in tempo, but one may point to a typical instance in chapter 20. Here Candide and his newfound companion Martin begin to discourse on the problem of evil. Voltaire provides a sample of their debate. It consists of four exchanges. The first two are brief. Candide wishes to know Martin's views; Martin replies that he is a Manichean. Candide registers astonishment; Martin says he cannot "think otherwise." Candide replies: "You must be possessed by the Devil" (202).

That unleashes a lengthy indictment by Martin of this evil world. It is one of the most trenchant summations in the whole *conte*. The Devil must be in charge, says Martin, when one sees that almost every town wants to destroy its neighbor, every family some other family; the weak curse the strong as they grovel before them, the strong treat the weak like sheep to be bought or sold. A million licensed murderers in uniform roam across Europe for want of a more decent calling, and even where peace and culture seem to reign, men are eaten up with envy and anxiety. Secret sorrows are even more cruel than public misfortune. All this is developed with rolling periods, in six sentences, building up to a climax in the fourth, which runs to 73 words, before ending on two brief statements: the first, about secret sorrows (11 words), and then the clinching remark, "In a word, I have seen and suffered so much that I am a Manichean" (202).

Voltaire closes the paragraph at that point. The following paragraph is just two lines forming an ironic coda. Candide attempts to reply to this onslaught: "However, there is some good" (202). He is cut down scathingly by Martin: it's possible, he says, but I don't know it. So ends the theoretical discussion. Voltaire immediately illustrates it in the next paragraph, whose brilliance can be appreciated only if we quote it in full:

> In the midst of this discussion, the sound of cannon is heard. The noise grows louder at every moment. Everyone picks up his telescope. Two ships are sighted, in combat about three miles away. The wind brings them so close to the French ship that one was able to enjoy watching the fight in comfort. At last, one of the two ships let loose on the other a broadside so low and accurate that it sent it to the bottom. Candide and Martin distinctly perceived a hundred men on the deck of the sinking ship; all of them were raising their hands to the sky and uttering fearful shouts; in an instant everything was swallowed up. (203)

Note the urgency of this description. The passage, of just over 100 words, contains seven sentences. The first six are simple; two of them consist of only one clause. The final sentence is longer. But, unlike the more sophisticated phraseology of Martin's speech, it is made up of three uncomplicated sections, in a ternary structure that is quite commonly found in Voltaire's style. The last of these is devastating.

Here is Voltaire's narration at his most laconic, providing only the barest details of the action. The only luxury permitted is the sardonic comment about the spectators watching "in comfort." The scene they are witnessing is one of horror; the wretched doomed men are praying and screaming, all to no avail. Again, Voltaire distances them from us. We are not to observe private tragedy or note the thoughts of a dying man. We are instead to look on at awful, collective horror, almost in the abstract, so to speak. (It is sometimes said that Voltaire anticipates cinematic techniques in *Candide;* here is surely a case in point, prefiguring filmed scenes of naval battle from the Second World War.) Nor is this the end of the episode. The spectacle is to be undercut by the ludicrous "miracle" that one of Candide's red sheep, stolen by Vanderdendur, escapes from the stricken vessel and rejoins him. Candide, despite what he has just seen, rejoices at the recovery of the lost sheep more than he had grieved over losing 100 of them—a clear parody of the New Testament parable about the lost sheep (Matthew 18; Luke 15)—and draws the pious conclusion that since the rascally Vanderdendur went down with the ship, crime is sometimes punished. The dramatic account of the naval battle is but the means to show up, before the episode is over, the abiding folly of human optimism.

To conclude this survey of the formal aspects of *Candide*, we must look more directly at Voltaire's language. This is best done by taking a passage and considering it in some detail; for even in translation one can gain some understanding of the particular qualities of Voltaire's prose. Let us, then, take the opening paragraph of chapter 3, where Voltaire memorably recounts the battle between the Bulgars and the Abars:

> Nothing was as beautiful, as sprightly, as brilliant, as well ordered as the two armies. The trumpets, fifes, oboes, drums, guns composed a harmony such as never was in Hell. The guns first of all knocked over approximately six thousand men on each side; next the musketry removed from the best of worlds around nine to ten thousand rascals who were infecting its surface. The bayonet was also the sufficient reason for the death of a few thousand men. The total could easily come to around thirty thousand souls. Candide, who was quaking like a philosopher, hid himself as best he could during this heroic butchery. (126)

This passage comes from the early chapters, where Voltaire is attacking Panglossian optimism directly. Hence the philosophical terms derived from Leibniz: "the best of worlds," "sufficient reason." These are exposed to the trenchant realities of war. Voltaire starts from a realistic account, then heightens it: artillery, infantry, bayonet. Only the cavalry is missing, perhaps because including it would have spoiled the ternary structure of which he was so fond.[4] The language is impeccably classical, and often euphemistic. But it is shot through from beginning to end with antithesis and paradox. The first sentence seems to admire the beauty and order of it all. One could just possibly imagine a military historian, say, ignoring the human dimension for the tactical, writing that sentence without irony. But the second sentence makes all clear. It too, at first, paints an attractive picture with all the military music. But the enumeration on this occasion, echoing that in the previous sentence, is subverted by the last detail (a common Voltairean practice, as we have already seen), when the guns are added to the musical instruments and the harmony, which would have fitted well with the Panglossian vision of the world, finds its comparison in Hell, not Heaven. Then comes the use of precise numbers, as if Voltaire were performing (just as with the Byng execution) a careful arithmetical exercise, arriving helpfully at an indication of the total numbers of the killed. Here too the emphasis is on the general scene: no blood or guts (that would have been stooping to vulgarity), no suffering, not even the screams and terror of the naval battle. It is an overview, from a distance. In one sense, it is a cruel depiction; but here as elsewhere, the reader is to infer the scandal of such a massacre. Finally, Voltaire foregrounds Candide. Here too, all is expressed in a mirror-image way. He has been a coward, like a philosopher—a clever play by Voltaire on the word. For philosophers were traditionally supposed to despise fear, as the Stoics and the Epicureans in their different ways had demonstrated. Yet on this abominable battlefield, any sensitive, and sensible, philosopher would have done exactly as Candide did in putting self-preservation ahead of disinterested reflection. So the scene reverts at the end to the collective view once again, and to this "heroic butchery" in parodic-heroic manner.

No single passage will convey the full richness of Voltairean style. This one, for instance, devotes little attention to Candide, so we get only the briefest glimpse of how Voltaire treats his hero in a sort of benevolent but distanced manner. But in terms of ironic undercutting of noble deeds by the application of a wrong word or phrase, it is a masterpiece of concision. The emphasis throughout is on disjunction, as befits a work satirizing a totally fallacious concept of cosmic order. Here is Voltaire at his wittiest. One may say that with some confidence, since Voltaire had, many years before, given an invaluable clue as to what he understood by wit. He put it thus:

> What is called wit is sometimes a new comparison, sometimes a subtle allusion; here the misuse of a word that one sets forth in one meaning but hints may have another; there a delicate link between two uncommon ideas; a striking metaphor; the search for what an object does not at first suggest but still effectively contains; the art of linking up two distant things or of dividing two things that seem to be united, or of opposing one to the other; the art of saying only half of what one thinks, so as to let it be guessed at.[5]

It is this view of art, laying stress upon disproportion, seeking ways to overturn received views of the world, and setting the thought at odds with the language expressing it, that underlies the paragraph describing the battle and, generally, the whole of *Candide.*

notes and references

Chapter 1

1. Alexander Pope, *Essay on Man*, ed. Maynard Mack (London: Methuen, 1950), 1:289–94.
2. Albert Camus, *L'Homme révolté* (Paris: Gallimard, 1952), especially chapters 1 and 2.
3. Voltaire, *Lettres philosophiques*, edited by Gustave Lanson and A. M. Rousseau (Paris: Didier, 1964), 2:139; hereafter cited in text.

Chapter 2

1. Aldous Huxley, *On the Margin* (New York: Doran, 1923), 21–22.
2. Voltaire, "[Ce monde-ci] subsiste de contradictions," in Deloffre and Van den Heuvel, 547.

Chapter 3

1. Pomeau, Introduction, 57.
2. *Année littéraire* 3 (1760): 165.
3. Quoted in *Voltaire's "Candide" and the Critics*, ed. M. P. Foster (Belmont, Calif.: Wadsworth, 1962), 90.
4. Madame de Staël, *De l'Allemagne*, ed. Jean de Pange and Simone Balayé (Paris: Hachette, 1958–60), 4:79.
5. Christopher Thacker, "Son of Candide," *Studies on Voltaire and the Eighteenth Century* (hereafter cited as *SV*) 58 (1967): 1515–31.
6. Jean Sareil, "Le Massacre de Voltaire dans les manuels scolaires," *SV* 212 (1982): 125–30.
7. René Pomeau, *La Religion de Voltaire*, 2d ed. (Paris: Nizet, 1969).
8. See p. ix. An earlier edition of the *Correspondence* edited by Besterman was published in Geneva by the Institut et Musée Voltaire (1953–65).
9. Jean Sareil, *Essai sur "Candide"* (Geneva: Droz, 1967), 104.

Chapter 4

1. Voltaire, *Essai sur les moeurs*, in Moland 12:419–20.
2. The resemblances between Eldorado and Pennsylvania were first explored in depth by W. H. Barber, "L'Angleterre dans *Candide*," *Revue de littérature comparée* 37 (1963): 202–15.

3. See René Pomeau, "La Référence allemande dans *Candide,*" in *Voltaire und Deutschland,* ed. Peter Brockmeier et al. (Stuttgart: Metzler, 1979), 170–72.

4. Christiane Mervaud, "Du carnaval au carnavalesque: l'épisode vénitien de *Candide,*" in *Le Siècle de Voltaire: Hommage à René Pomeau,* ed. Christiane Mervaud and Sylvain Menant (Oxford: Voltaire Foundation, 1987), 651–62.

Chapter 5

1. Voltaire, *Dictionnaire philosophique,* in Moland, 18:127.

2. See Haydn Mason, *Pierre Bayle and Voltaire* (Oxford: Oxford University Press, 1963), 67–77, and "Voltaire and Manichean Dualism," *SV* 26 (1963): 1143–60.

3. George R. Havens, *Voltaire's Marginalia on the Pages of Rousseau* (Columbus: Ohio State University Press, 1933), 15.

4. Voltaire, *Poème sur le désastre de Lisbonne,* in Moland 9:477.

5. In view of the parallels noted earlier with Beckett's *Godot,* it is interesting to observe that the phrase "O che sciagura d'essere senza c . . . !" is used by Beckett on a number of occasions. The matter is briefly discussed in John Fletcher, *The Novels of Samuel Beckett* (London: Chatto and Windus, 1964), 20.

6. Albert Camus, *The Myth of Sisyphus* (Paris: Gallimard, 1942), 19 and *passim.*

7. One of the most persuasive of such commentators in recent times is Jacques Van den Heuvel, *Voltaire dans ses contes* (Paris: Colin, 1967), 261.

8. J. G. Weightman, "The Quality of *Candide,*" in *Essays Presented to C. M. Girdlestone,* ed. E. T. Dubois et al. (Newcastle-upon-Tyne: King's College, 1960), 338, 340, 346.

9. *La Métaphysique de Newton* (1740), in Moland 22:407.

10. Roy S. Wolper, "Candide: Gull in the Garden?" *Eighteenth-Century Studies* 3 (1969–70): 268; hereafter cited in text.

11. See, for example, Theodore E. D. Braun, "Voltaire and His *Contes:* A Review Essay on Interpretations Offered by Roy S. Wolper," *SV* 212 (1982) 311–17, 328–30; hereafter cited in text.

12. A useful discussion of this aspect has been provided by C. J. Betts, "On the Beginning and Ending of *Candide,*" *Modern Language Review* 80 (1985): 283–92.

13. Gustave Flaubert, letter to Louise de Cormenin, 7 June 1844, cited in Van den Heuvel, *Voltaire,* 277 (Flaubert's emphasis).

14. André Magnan, *Candide* (Paris: Presses Universitaires de France, 1987), 95–96.

15. *Romans et contes de Voltaire,* ed. Roland Barthes, 2 vols. (Paris: Club des Libraires de France, 1958), 28, cited in Van den Heuvel, *Voltaire,* 277.

16. René Pomeau traces the known history of the circumstances surrounding Voltaire's birth in *D'Arouet à Voltaire* (Oxford: Voltaire Foundation,

1985), 17–27. The working out of this personal situation in Voltaire's writings is traced in José-Michel Moureaux, "L'*Oedipe* de Voltaire: Introduction à une psycholecture," *Archives des lettres modernes* 146 (1973); René Pomeau, "Voltaire et Shakespeare: Du Père justicier au Père assassiné," in *Mélanges offerts au Professeur René Fromilhague, Littératures* (Toulouse, 1984), 99–106; Mason, "Fathers, Good and Bad, in Voltaire's *Mahomet*," in *Myth and Its Making in the French Theatre: Studies Presented to W. D. Howarth* (Cambridge: Cambridge University Press, 1988), 121–35.

17. Pomeau notes that the incident is reminiscent of an actual happening when Voltaire was still at the court of Frederick the Great, and suspects an ironic intent behind it (124, n6).

Chapter 6

1. *Candide, ou l'optimisme*, ed. Christopher Thacker (Geneva: Droz, 1968), 48.

2. See D-1391. (Voltaire, letter to Bonaventure Moussinot, 17 November [1737]); the phraseology is virtually parallel.

3. This point is made by Vivienne Mylne in a useful article, "A *Pícara* in *Candide:* Paquette," *College Literature* 6 (1979–80): 205–10.

4. Cf. page 23 of this volume.

5. Genesis 2:15, translated in the King James version as "to dress it and to keep it."

6. See René Pomeau, "La Référence allemande dans *Candide*," in Brockmeier, *Voltaire und Deutschland*, esp. 170–72.

7. Cf. pages 72–73 of this volume.

8. Cf. page 40 of this volume.

9. Donna Dalnekoff neatly points out that the Oreillons spare Candide only because he is able to prove to them that he is a murderer. "The Meaning of Eldorado: Utopia and Satire in *Candide*," *SV* 127 (1974):48.

10. Cf. page 51 of this volume.

11. Cf. page 27 of this volume.

12. It should be noted that there is no mention of this infidelity in the original 1759 version. Evidently Voltaire felt it to be merely one more satiric blow to aim at the corruption of Paris, not a matter of fundamental consequence. Candide, of course, never asks Cunégonde's pardon when he finds her; but by then horror at her ugliness predominates.

13. Voltaire uses a similar form of words about the French nation in *L'Ingénu* (1767): "C'est donc ainsi qu'on traite les hommes comme des singes! On les bat et on les fait danser" (So that is how they treat men like monkeys! They beat them and make them dance). Deloffre and Van den Heuvel, 344.

Chapter 7

1. René Pomeau, *La Religion de Voltaire* (Paris: Nizet, 1969) 369.

2. Antoine François Prévost d'Exiles, *Manon Lescaut,* ed. Fréderic Deloffre and Raymond Picard (Paris: Garnier, 1965), 44.

3. Voltaire, *Zadig,* Deloffre and Van den Heuvel, 57.

4. Cf. Pomeau, 126, n. 1; cf. pages 21–22 in this volume for a suggestion that Voltaire may have been influenced by a letter he received describing the battle of Rossbach.

5. Voltaire, *Dictionnaire philosophique,* art, "Esprit," section première (*Lettre sur l'esprit,* 1744) in Moland 19:3.

selected bibliography

PRIMARY WORKS

Brumfitt, J. H., ed. *Candide.* Oxford: Oxford University Press, 1971. Most useful of the popular editions in English. Especially helpful on the ideas in *Candide.*

Magnan, André, ed. *Candide, ou l'optimisme.* Paris: Presses Universitaires de France, 1987. An edition intended mainly for French undergraduates. Perceptive notably where matters of form are concerned.

Morize, André, ed. *Candide, ou l'optimisme,* 2d ed. Paris: Didier, 1957. The most complete edition in terms of documentation. Remains an invaluable source of reference for all studies of *Candide.*

Pomeau, René, ed. *Candide, ou l'optimisme.* Vol 48 of *The Complete Works of Voltaire.* Oxford: Voltaire Foundation, 1980. The currently authoritative edition.

Thacker, Christopher, ed. *Candide, ou l'optimisme.* Geneva: Droz, 1968. Especially valuable for its critical introduction, particularly on themes in *Candide,* and the section on sources of the *conte.*

Wade, Ira O. *Voltaire and "Candide."* Princeton: Princeton University Press, 1959. Particularly interesting for being the first study to include and discuss the only existing manuscript version of *Candide* as a whole.

Other Voltaire Works

Besterman, Theodore, ed. *Voltaire's Correspondence.* Vols. 85–135 of *The Complete Works of Voltaire.* Geneva and Banbury, England: Voltaire Foundation, 1968–75.

Deloffre, Frédéric, and Jacques Van den Heuvel, eds. *Voltaire: Romans et contes.* Paris: Gallimard, 1979. *L'Ingénu,* 285–347; *Zadig,* 55–123.

Lanson, Gustave, and A. M. Rousseau, eds. *Lettres philosophiques,* 2 vols. (Paris: Didier, 1964).

Moland, Louis, ed. *Oeuvres complètes.* 52 vols. Paris: Garnier, 1877–85. *Dictionnaire philosophique,* vols. 17–21; *Discours en vers sur l'homme,* vol. 9, 378–428; *Essai sur les moeurs,* vols. 11, 12, and 13, 1–184; *La Métaphysique de Newton,* in *Eléments de Philosophe de Newton,* part 1, vol. 22, 403–37; *Poème sur le désastre de Lisbonne,* vol. 9, 465–80.

SECONDARY WORKS

Books

Note: *SV = Studies on Voltaire and the Eighteenth Century.*

Barber, W. H. *Voltaire: "Candide."* London: Arnold, 1960. Still the most reliable brief account in English, with a particularly useful discussion of Voltaire's views on optimism.

Bottiglia, W. F. *Voltaire's Candide,* rev. ed. *SV* 7A. Geneva: Institut et Musée Voltaire, 1964. The first book-length account of *Candide,* treating all aspects of the work.

Foster, M. P., ed. *Voltaire's "Candide" and the Critics.* Belmont, Calif.: Wadsworth, 1962.

Magnan, André. *Voltaire: Candide ou l'optimisme.* Paris: Presses Universitaires de France, 1987. Penetrating analysis of *Candide* as narrative artifact.

Sareil, Jean. *Essai sur "Candide."* Geneva: Droz, 1967. Lively and stimulating. One of the first critics to argue that *Candide* is neither metaphysical nor didactic but primarily a comic masterpiece.

Waldinger, Renée, ed. *Approaches to Teaching Candide.* New York: Modern Language Association, 1987. Helpful essays by teachers on their aims and experiences when presenting *Candide* in the classroom.

Articles and Parts of Books

Barber, W. H. "L'Angleterre dans *Candide.*" *Revue de littérature comparée* 37 (1963): 202–15. Inter alia, shows that Eldorado is to some extent fashioned from Voltaire's views on Pennsylvania.

Betts, C. J. "On the Beginning and Ending of *Candide.*" *Modern Language Review* 80 (1985): 283–92. Sees interesting structural parallels between the first and last chapters.

Braun, Theodore E. D. "Voltaire and His *Contes:* A Review Essay on Interpretations Offered by Roy S. Wolper." *SV* 212 (1982): 311–17, 328–30. An interesting defense of Wolper's views (see below).

Brooks, Richard A. "Voltaire and Garcilaso de la Vega." *SV* 30 (1964): 189–204. Reveals a documentary source for the Oreillons and Eldorado episodes.

Dalnekoff, Donna Isaacs. "The Meaning of Eldorado: Utopia and Satire in *Candide.*" *SV* 127 (1974): 41–59. Argues that Eldorado, far from being a model, is mocked as an impossible ideal.

Gilot, Michel. "Le Cycle des semaines dans *Candide.*" In *Lettres et réalités: Mélanges de littérature générale et de critique romanesque offerts au Professeur Henri Coulet par ses amis,* 117–29. Aix-en-Provence: Université de Provence, 1988. Illuminating observations on the structure of the *conte.*

Henry, Patrick. "Sacred and Profane Gardens in *Candide*." *SV* 176 (1979): 133–52. One of the most penetrating investigations of the garden motif in the *conte*.

Howells, R. J. " 'Cette Boucherie Héroïque': *Candide* as Carnival." *Modern Language Review* 80 (1985): 293–303. Fruitfully Bakhtinian approach to the tale.

Langdon, David. "On the Meanings of the Conclusion of *Candide*." *SV* 238 (1985): 397–432. Descries a purposeful tone to the ending.

Leigh, R. A. "From the *Inégalité* to *Candide*: Notes on a Desultory Dialogue between Rousseau and Voltaire (1755–59)." In *The Age of Enlightenment: Studies Presented to Theodore Besterman*, edited by W. H. Barber et al., 66–92. Edinburgh: Oliver and Boyd, 1967. Sets *Candide* in the context of Voltaire's relations with Rousseau at the time, treating skeptically Rousseau's claim to have inspired the *conte* as a reply to his own essay on inequality, but arguing that "Voltaire had Rousseau in mind rather more than has sometimes been supposed."

Mason, Haydn. "Conteur." In *Voltaire*, 57–73. London: Hutchinson, 1975. A general account of Voltaire's tales.

———. "Geneva and *Candide*." In *Voltaire: A Biography*, 70–92. London: Granada, 1981. Looks at *Candide* in the context of Voltaire's life.

———. "Voltaire's '*Contes*': An 'Etat Présent.' " *Modern Language Review* 65 (1970): 19–35. General survey of writings on Voltaire's *contes* up to 1970.

Mervaud, Christiane. "Du carnaval au carnavalesque: l'épisode vénitien de *Candide*." In *Le Siècle de Voltaire: Hommage à René Pomeau*, edited by Christiane Mervaud and Sylvain Menant, 651–62. Oxford: Voltaire Foundation, 1987. Convincingly demonstrates that the section on Venice encapsulates the essentially ironic vision of the whole work.

Murray, Geoffrey. "Voltaire's *Candide*: The Protean Gardener, 1755–62." *SV* 69. Geneva: Institut en Musée Voltaire, 1970. Interestingly relates the genesis of the *conte* to Voltaire's own correspondence of the period.

Mylne, Vivienne. "Wolper's View of Voltaire's Tales." *SV* 212 (1982): 318–27. Takes a generally unfavorable view of Wolper's views (see below).

Pomeau, René. "Candide entre Marx et Freud." *SV* 89 (1972): 1305–23. A searching inquiry into the attitudes displayed in *Candide* toward work and sex.

Starobinski, Jean. "*Candide* et la question de l'autorité." In *Essays on the Age of Enlightenment in Honor of Ira O. Wade*, edited by Jean Macary, 305–12. Geneva: Droz, 1977. Masterly presentation of the ways in which the principle of authority is repeatedly undermined in the story.

———. "Sur le style philosophique de *Candide*." *Comparative Literature* 28 (1976): 193–200. Richly stimulating essay, bringing out a keen sense of the fundamentally ironic mode of *Candide*.

Stavan, H. A. "Are Voltaire's Tales Narrative Fantasies? A Reply to Wolper." *SV* 215 (1982): 281–87. Another critical attitude toward the Wolper thesis (see below).

Thacker, Christopher. "Son of Candide." *SV* 58 (1967): 1515–31. A survey of the imitations of the *conte* that appeared up to 1804.

Torrey, Norman L. "Candide's Garden and the Lord's Vineyard." *SV* 27 (1963): 1657–66. From an analysis of Voltaire's correspondence, concludes on a pessimistic reading of *Candide.*

Van den Heuvel, Jacques. *Voltaire dans ses contes,* 236–91. Paris: Colin, 1967. Though occasionally overinclined to discern Voltaire's personal life in his tales, contains a wealth of pertinent observations, especially on the thematic developments.

Weightman, J. G. "The Quality of *Candide.*" In *Essays Presented to C. M. Girdlestone,* edited by E. T. Dubois et al., 335–47. Newcastle-upon-Tyne: King's College, 1960. Reprinted in *Candide: Or, Optimism,* edited by Robert M. Adams, 151–64. New York: Norton, 1966. Trenchantly seizes upon what the author sees as the tragicomic, dialectical tone of the tale.

Wolper, Roy S. "Candide: Gull in the Garden?" *Eighteenth-Century Studies* 3 (1969–70): 265–77. Important revisionist article on *Candide* that has stimulated a lively controversy on the meaning of this and other stories by Voltaire. See Braun (1982), Mylne (1982), and Stavan (1982).

index

Index

the author

Haydn Mason, Professor of French at the University of Bristol, is the author of several books and articles on Voltaire, as well as on other French writers of the seventeenth and eighteenth centuries. He is the current President of the International Society for Eighteenth-Century Studies and is Chair of the Board of Directors for the Voltaire Foundation at the University of Oxford. He has held chairs at a number of universities, including the University of East Anglia, the University of Maryland, and the Université de Paris-III (Sorbonne Nouvelle).